Praise for
TAKE UP SPACE, Y'ALL

"Tess Holliday is someone I've long admired for how she shows up in the world for herself and others by pushing boundaries and trailblazing new paths for all of us. *Take Up Space, Y'all* is an unapologetic anthem to discovering and celebrating all of the facets of ourselves and to nourishing our continued evolution. Together, Tess and Kelly have crafted a powerful and important book."

—Mandy Moore, singer-songwriter and actress

"Gosh, I love this book . . . If only I had it when I was growing up! Written in a language and tone that is like having a conversation with your bestie who loves you to bits (and also happens to know a ton more than you do), Tess's vibrant spirit spills out of the pages, encouraging us to stop putting our trust and focus outside of ourselves, and instead to look inward. From debunking social media to giving solid guidance for self-care and confidence-building, Tess reminds us that we all have our own unique, great-big-beautiful soul that deserves to shine. And the moment we stop trying to shove ourselves into a mold that isn't made for us, that's when we start to soar."

—Elisa Donovan, actress from *Clueless* and *Sabrina the Teenage Witch*, and author of *Wake Me When You Leave*

"Tess Holliday and Kelly Coon's wonderfully practical and brilliantly informative book is pitch perfectly age-appropriate and incredibly fun! It encourages the reader to look at their developing selves and navigate new situations with curiosity, creativity and a deep sense of kindness for themselves and the rest of the world."

—Melanie Zanetti, award-winning actress and voice-over artist

"This is the book I wish I'd had when I was navigating adolescence. Every page is bursting with helpful, practical tips, beautiful insights on living your best life inside and out, and plenty of humor. Make space for this one on every young person's bookshelf. Fresh, fabulous, and fun."

—Laura Taylor Namey, *New York Times* bestselling author of *A Cuban Girl's Guide to Tea and Tomorrow*

TAKE UP SPACE, Y'ALL

YOUR BOLD & BRIGHT GUIDE TO SELF-LOVE

TESS HOLLIDAY & KELLY COON

SUPERMODEL AND BODY ACTIVIST

RP | TEENS
PHILADELPHIA

Running Press Teens
Hachette Book Group
1290 Avenue of the Americas, New York, NY 10104
www.runningpresskids.com
@runningpresskids

First Edition: August 2025

Published by Running Press Teens, an imprint of Hachette Book Group, Inc. The Running Press Teens name and logo are trademarks of Hachette Book Group, Inc.

The Hachette Speakers Bureau provides a wide range of authors for speaking events. To find out more, go to www.hachettespeakersbureau.com or email HachetteSpeakers@hbgusa.com.

Running Press books may be purchased in bulk for business, educational, or promotional use. For more information, please contact your local bookseller or the Hachette Book Group Special Markets Department at Special.Markets@hbgusa.com.

The publisher is not responsible for websites (or their content) that are not owned by the publisher.

Print book cover and interior design by Frances J. Soo Ping Chow
Photographs on pp viii, xiv, and 72 by Bonnie Nichoalds
Stock illustrations copyright © GettyImages

Library of Congress Cataloging-in-Publication Data
Names: Holliday, Tess, author. | Coon, Kelly, author.
Title: Take up space, y'all : your bold & bright guide to self-love /
Tess Holliday, supermodel and body activist & Kelly Coon.
Description: First edition. | Philadelphia : RP Teens, 2025. |
Audience term: Teenagers | Audience: Ages 12 & up | Audience: Grades 7–9
Identifiers: LCCN 2024041403 (print) | LCCN 2024041404 (ebook) |
ISBN 9780762489152 (paperback) | ISBN 9780762489169 (ebook)
Subjects: LCSH: Self-esteem—Juvenile literature. |
Self-acceptance—Juvenile literature. | Body image—Juvenile literature.
Classification: LCC BF697.5.S46 H645 2025 (print) | LCC BF697.5.S46 (ebook) |
DDC 650.1—dc23/eng/20250209
LC record available at https://lccn.loc.gov/2024041403
LC ebook record available at https://lccn.loc.gov/2024041404

ISBNs: 978-0-7624-8915-2 (paperback), 978-0-7624-8916-9 (ebook)

Printed in Indiana, USA

LSC-C

Printing 1, 2025

For my younger self,
who navigated the twists and
turns of childhood
with a heart full of wonder and
an unbreakable spirit.

—T. H.

For Terri Gatz and Terriee Smith,
two bright women
who saw the light in me.

—K. C.

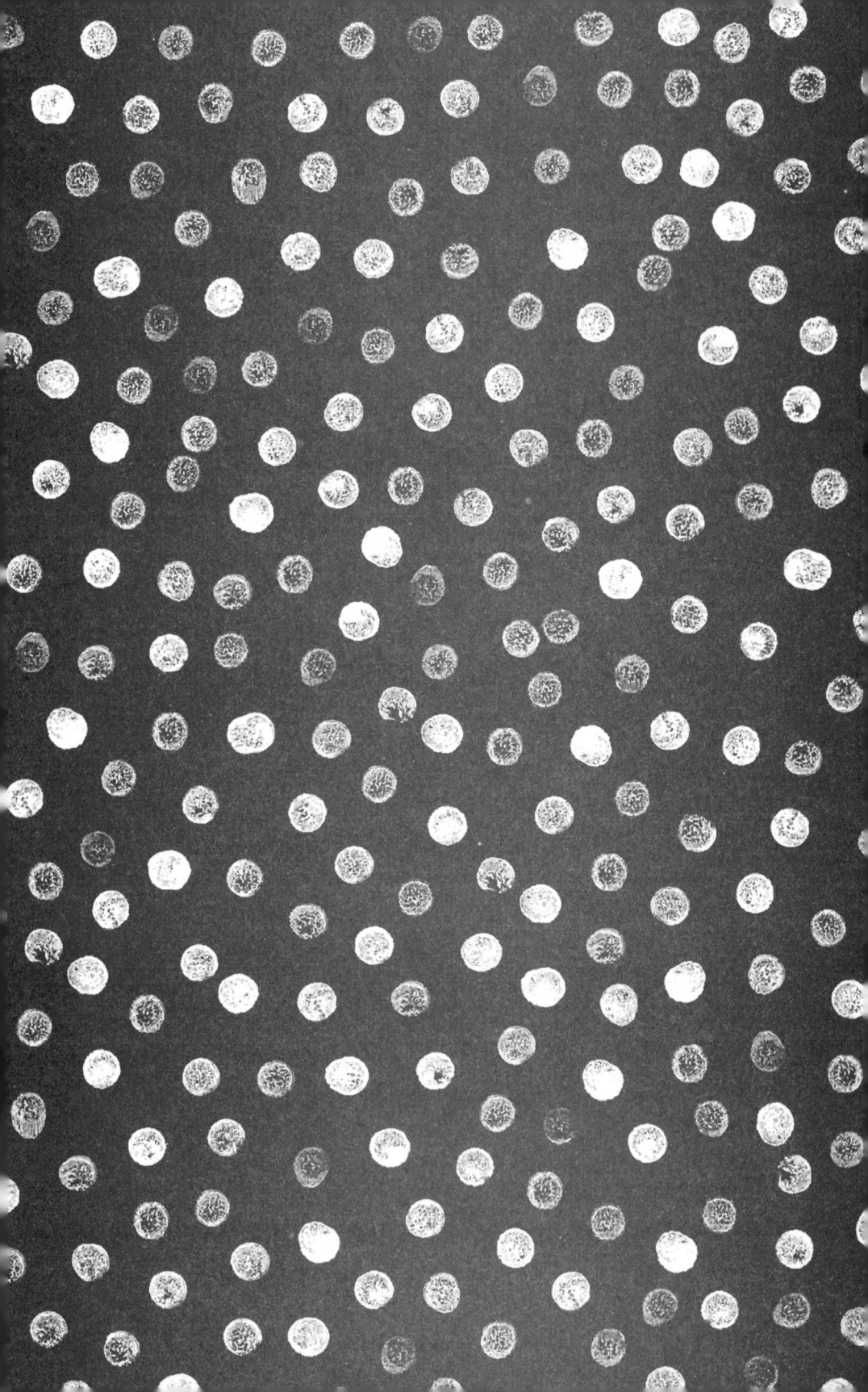

Contents

Introduction:
GET TO KNOW TESS HOLLIDAY

*H*ey y'all! Tess here. I wanted to personally say thank you for coming along on this ride with Kelly and me. We're excited to have you share some time with us! =) Listen in while we chat a little bit about why we chose to write this book and what you can expect to see inside. Stay amazing!

XO *Tess*

KELLY: Hey Tess! Thanks for taking some of your incredibly busy time handling life like a BOSS to write this book with me! I'm honored and thrilled (aka screaming, crying, all the starry-eyed reactions). Will you introduce yourself to our lovely readers? Tell us a few things about what makes you *you*?

TESS: Ugh, I'm so bad at talking about myself.

KELLY: Haha, same. Just speak from your heart. That's all we want.

TESS: I wear a lot of hats. I'm a mom. I'm the founder of Eff Your Beauty Standards, which was one of the first viral body-positive movements. I'm a model. I'm a diversity and inclusivity consultant for H&M and other brands. You know. I do some things.

KELLY: Some *things*? Haven't you been on a zillion magazine covers? *Self*, *Cosmo*, *People*, *Nylon*, *Parents*, etc.? Haven't you been on *Good Morning America*, the *Today* show, I don't know . . . a whole bucketload of others? You're wildly impressive.

TESS: I mean, thank you, and sure, yes, I have done all these things, but I was also once just a kid who was bullied and picked apart for the way that I existed in the world. I've made a career for myself despite people putting me in a box and doubting what I was capable of. Maybe because of it. That girl is never far from my mind.

KELLY: Wanna talk about her? That girl? Where is she from? Where did she go to high school?

TESS: Well, in Laurel, Mississippi, in an abandoned Walmart. True story.

KELLY: Ha! Really? A Walmart? Were the signs still up? Like did you go to Chemistry in Electronics and Geometry in Lawn and Garden?

TESS: Hahaha—kind of! I mean, I actually ate lunch in the Lawn and Garden section outside.

KELLY: No, you did *not*.

TESS: Oh, we did. West Jones High School. It's still there! You can look it up. The rooms were all built out of plywood so the whole place smelled like sawdust.

And there were no ceilings to the classrooms either, because they only built the walls high enough to separate us. So we would throw notes and paper airplanes over the wall to each other. You know. Before *cell phones*.

KELLY: Oh, I remember those days well.

TESS: It was weird and wild, but, you know, it was still a high school. Still all the pressure. The drama. The angst. All of that.

KELLY: I bet. Teens are pressured about everything, right? If it's not grades, it's looks. If it's not looks, it's achievement—

TESS: —or social media pressure or relationships.

KELLY: Exactly. What were some of the biggest pressures *you* faced in high school?

TESS: I think most of the pressure had to do with my size and not having a lot of money. When I was younger, it was about my mom being disabled. I remember very distinctly my mom taking me to a new school the first day of fifth grade. My classmates were making fun of her being in a wheelchair.

KELLY: Awful.

TESS: It was. Before then I had never really been bullied. So that was kind of my first introduction to it. But as I got older, most of the stuff was about my weight. My status.

KELLY: How did you deal with it back then?

TESS: At first, I buried myself in things I liked to do. I sang in The Singers, which was what we called chorus. I was an alto, and we practiced in the loading docks.

KELLY: Of course you did.

TESS: Haha, yes. *Walmart* I'd sing and hear it echo off the walls and the chain-link fencing and kind of escape into my head and let it all go. But, you know, even that wasn't perfect. My outfits all had to be custom made when we performed. Different materials, different shapes. It made me stick out and feel uncomfortable. That's why size inclusivity is *so, so* important to me now. Kids should *never* feel the way I felt when I was just trying to do something I loved.

KELLY: Do you sing now? Are you going to add "famous singer" to your long list of accomplishments?

TESS: Haha! The world isn't ready for my Paris Hilton "Stars Are Blind" moment.

KELLY: Okay, but *I* am.

TESS: Then you'll have to come over for karaoke night.

KELLY: Don't threaten me with a good time. So you never became a singer, but you *did* become a model. Will you walk me through the day you answered a casting call for modeling when you were fifteen?

TESS: Yeah, sure! So my mom and I were riding around in the car, and we heard an ad on the radio about a casting call in Atlanta, Georgia, for plus-sized models. And I remember hearing that and thinking to myself, *Plus-sized models are a thing?* I told my mom right then that I wanted to do it. I remember thinking, *I'm gonna go there and I'm gonna get signed. It's destiny.* Meanwhile, we had no money at all. *No* money. But I wanted headshots and my mom believed in me, so we got this photographer in our small town to take pictures of me for the casting call. He shot these hilarious photos that I still have. I've got on white eyeliner and cow-print platforms. It was a *sight.*

KELLY: Oh, that's absolutely darling.

TESS: Anyway, a couple of weeks later my mom and her husband at the time scraped enough cash together—I still have no idea how she did it— to drive me six or seven hours to the nicest hotel I'd ever seen where the casting call was. There were thirty-plus agencies there, including Ford Models. I had to walk a runway. I did all the little workshops they had. Even yoga.

KELLY: And did you get signed?

TESS: I got exactly *one* call back from Frontier Booking Agency. But you know what? I was thrilled that I'd even gotten that. So I went to his little table all excited, but I'll never forget what he said to me: "Listen, the best that you can ever hope for at your height and size"—I was a size sixteen and 5'3" at that point—"is catalog work." So I didn't sign with him because I wanted more.

KELLY: How did you get more? How did you achieve your dream of becoming a model?

TESS: I followed my heart. I became a makeup artist, which was something I was always into, and though I heard that guy's voice in my head whenever someone told me I was too short or too fat to model, eventually I moved to LA and answered another casting call. I scored my first ad campaign and ended up on billboards and in every major magazine. It grew and grew from there.

KELLY: Wow. I'm so glad you never let that guy make you quit!

TESS: If anything, it pushed me harder. I'm proud that I never gave up.

KELLY: What are you *most* proud of, though? Professionally speaking?

TESS: Honestly, I'm proud of my contribution to making the world a better and safer place for folks in larger bodies. I can say that I'm part of a collective of people who have helped shift a generation. I look around now at fashion and media and see how much it's changed since I was a kid in The Singers, unable to find clothes that fit. I can drive down Sunset Boulevard and see plus-sized models in ad campaigns for all kinds of brands. Knowing that I had a hand in helping to open the doors for other people to feel seen and heard is really meaningful.

KELLY: Dang. I have goosebumps.

TESS: Haha, me too. I still sometimes pinch myself that I have this platform. I get to support myself and family doing something I love. One of the wildest moments for me was seeing myself on the cover of *People* magazine. I grew up reading my mom's old *People* issues on the couch. When she got her copy with my face on the cover, it made me remember just how far I'd come.

KELLY: What an incredible feeling. Is that why you wanted to write this book with me? To give hope to kids who might be doubting their own self-worth or are being hard on themselves?

TESS: Absolutely. I grew up before Lizzo. There were no positive plus-sized role models telling kids who fell outside the norm that they were just fine exactly how they were. I spent years of my life trying to fit in and found real success when I stopped doing that. This book helps young people know that their lives don't have to start when they look the way they think they should look or have the right amount of money or fit into a certain standard that society has just come up with. They can live well right now, just as they are.

KELLY: What would you say to the teen who is reading this? That kid who might not believe that they're good enough?

TESS: Don't shrink yourself. Whether metaphorically or physically or any other way, you can live life to the fullest by taking up all the space you need.

KELLY: Wow. I'm going to go ahead and tattoo that on my forehead so I never ever forget.

TESS: Haha, okay, me too. One more can't hurt.

KELLY: And we're going to talk about all those tattoos soon! First, though, we'll give our readers insider tips about loving who they are on the outside, right? Everything from handling backhanded compliments to managing skincare to getting rid of social standards that don't agree with who we are.

TESS: Exactly. Then we'll talk about some of the trickier stuff, like dropping toxic relationships, dealing with social media, claiming labels, and battling our inner critics because we're done with self-shame this year. D-O-N-E.

KELLY: Oooh, can't wait! Thanks for chatting with me, Tess. You're the best.

TESS: Anytime. XO

PART 1

LOVE YOUR OUTER YOU

"YOU'RE WORTH SHOWING UP FOR. ADVOCATING FOR. FIGHTING FOR."

—TESS HOLLIDAY

CHAPTER 1

FIND YOUR FIT

HAVE YOU EVER LOOKED BACK AT CLOTHING STYLES IN THE United States from 150 years ago and thought to yourself, *Absolutely not!?* Everything was so *proper*, wasn't it? Corset waists and ankle-covering skirts for the women. Suits and hats for the men, even if they didn't have anything more spectacular to do that day than plow a field or write a letter to their great-aunt Agatha.

Wild.

Today we have more options, praise to the gods of buttons and bustles. If you want to wear a long skirt and pointy little boots to class, knock yourself out. If you want to wear a three-piece suit to walk the dog, you do you. If you want to wear a T-shirt and pair of sweatpants every day for the rest of your life, you probably can (unless you're attending the funeral for your great-aunt Agatha, in which case, dress up a little. She's *family*.). The point is: you have options. You can, unless you've been given a dress code, choose how to drape your body as long as you keep all the important bits covered when they need to be.

Dress Codes 101

Dress codes aren't just a school thing. Sometimes you'll be asked to dress a particular way for a wedding, a dance, a job, or even your great-aunt Agatha's funeral, so it's good to know your options if your mom says, "No, you can't wear your Metallica concert T-shirt! It's a formal event!" Even if you're *not* told what to wear, it can be good to know what other people might be wearing wherever you're going, especially if you're the type of person who prefers to blend in.

3

DRESS CODE LEVEL*	OCCASIONS WHERE YOU MIGHT WEAR THIS STUFF	CLOTHES YOU COULD CHOOSE
CASUAL: Whatever is clean and comfy.	Family barbecue, school, hanging out with friends	T-shirt, shorts, jeans, sweats, sweatshirt, skirt (you name it)
BUSINESS OR DRESSY CASUAL: Kick it up a notch.	An interview, an important meeting, a date, a wedding if it's outdoors or the invitation specifies	A collared shirt, khakis, a dress or skirt and fancy top; boat shoes, nice gym shoes, sandals, or dress shoes
SEMI-FORMAL: Gotta look sharp!	Homecoming, a wedding, a funeral, a milestone birthday party for an important adult in your life	A cocktail or formal dress (depending on the occasion); collared, long-sleeved shirt and tie, slacks, a blazer; nice dress shoes, dressy heels, or flats
FORMAL: Dress to the nines.	Prom, a wedding, a gala	A suit and tie or tuxedo, a floor-length gown or glam cocktail dress, a fancy pantsuit; dressiest dress shoes
BLACK TIE: Go all out!	A super-fancy wedding, a major fundraiser, a huge awards ceremony	A tuxedo and patent-leather dress shoes; a ball gown and glam shoes

Please note that these levels and clothing suggestions might not apply given your culture or religion, so when in doubt, ask that one cousin of yours who knows everything.

I Can Wear What I Like . . . But What Do I Like?

For some people, clothes shopping is *amazing*. They love wandering through the mall or the local thrift store with an armload of clothes and a blissful afternoon to try everything on. For others, even the idea of stepping foot in a store makes them sweat because they have no money for new clothes, no idea what looks good, or no idea of what they even like.

Unleash Your Own Style

Style, according to fashion designer Tan France, is personal. It's not about following every trend or shopping at certain stores; it's figuring out how to express yourself by pulling together clothes, shoes, and accessories. It's about matching your outside to your inside.

When Tess was growing up, there weren't that many plus-sized clothing options for teenagers. One of the only stores that even sold stuff in her size was Lane Bryant, which would have been great if she'd wanted to look like a thirteen-year-old bank teller. Because of that, she didn't get to figure out her personal style until she was older. But you can determine your personal style right now! Tess has developed a method with four ridiculously easy steps to help.

STEP 1:
FIND YOUR STARTING POINT

Dig into your closet. You probably have a few items that you absolutely *love* to wear. Maybe it's a concert T-shirt and an incredible pair of kicks. Or maybe it's some jeans and an old jacket your grandpa used to wear. Whatever it is, there's a reason you like that stuff. See if you can find commonalities among the pieces. Is it the fit you're drawn to? Silhouette? Comfort? Color? Nostalgia? What makes you love them?

STEP 2:
DREAM BIG

On socials, follow people—maybe actors, fashion bloggers, influencers, musicians, or community leaders—who dress in an interesting or inspirational way. Screenshot some of your favorite outfits. You could make a mood board or save links in a platform like Pinterest.

STEP 3:
PLAY AROUND

Inspired by those pictures, put outfits together using some of the favorites from your own closet. Maybe you can create brand-new looks just by pairing things differently. Or maybe you only need a necklace or a particular shirt to put the whole thing together.

STEP 4:
STEP OUTSIDE THE BOX

Finally, try new things! When you go shopping, keep your favorites and your inspiration photos in mind, but let yourself run wild too. Did you find a hot-pink jacket with lightning bolts in a bargain bin that you love even though nobody else in your friend group will? Who cares. Buy it anyway. Love floral headscarves? Throw 'em on. Your style can be as individual as you are, no matter what the haters might say.

**THREE WAYS TO RESPOND IF
SOMEONE IS MEAN ABOUT YOUR CLOTHES:**

1. "I'm sorry. I didn't catch that. Will you repeat it?" Asking for a repeat takes all the fun out of the dig for them. Explaining a joke ruins it every time.

2. "Were you *trying* to be rude when you said that about my outfit?" If they say no, then go, "Weird. It came out that way."

3. If they follow it up with "I was just joking," say, with a completely deadpan expression, "Get better at comedy" or "Cool," with a thumbs-up.

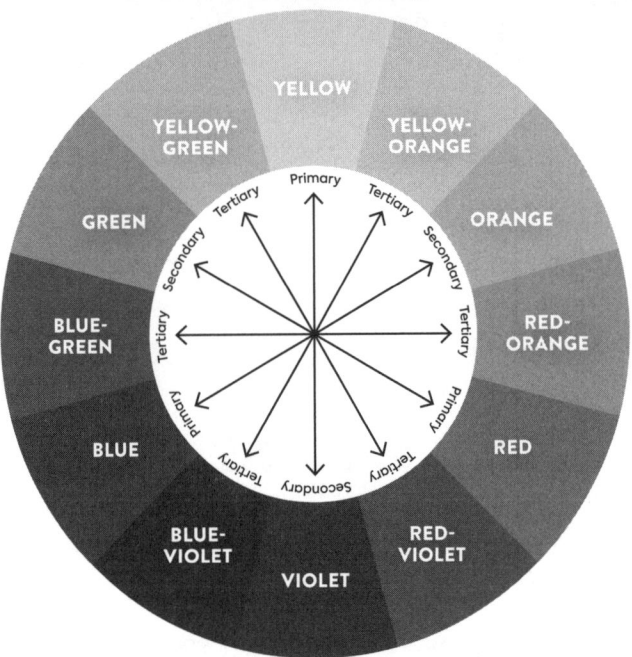

Spinning the Color Wheel

Let's revisit that amazing hot-pink lightning-bolt jacket you found. What if every time you pull it out of your closet, you have no idea what to wear with it? Welp, let's chat about colors that coordinate, shall we?

The **primary colors** that we all learned in kindergarten are *yellow*, *red*, and *blue*. When you mix two primary colors, you get the **secondary colors**: *violet*, *orange*, and *green*. When you mix a secondary color with a primary color, you get the **tertiary colors**: *red-violet*, *red-orange*, *yellow-orange*, *yellow-green*, *blue-green*, and *blue-violet*.

Got it? Great! But what does that have to do with clothes? Lots!

When you're choosing an outfit:

- **CHOOSE COLORS THAT ARE ANALOGOUS:** Analogous colors sit next to each other on the color wheel and share a common hue or tone. For example, red-violet, red, and violet are all analogous. So if you wanna wear your hot-pink (red-violet) jacket, maybe mix it with a violet T-shirt. They'll look good together because they're in the same color family.

- **CHOOSE COLORS THAT ARE COMPLEMENTARY:** Complementary colors are opposite from each other on the color wheel and tend to pair nicely. Your hot-pink jacket might go well with a yellowish-green tank dress and white Chuck Taylors, for example. A yellow sweatshirt might make your violet track pants stand out.

- **CHOOSE NEUTRALS:** The neutrals—white, tan, black, and denim—are always a safe bet. If you don't have anything else that goes with a stand-out piece like your lightning-bolt jacket, choose a white T-shirt and a pair of jeans, and call it a day.

- **CHOOSE COLORS YOU SIMPLY LIKE:** If *you* like certain colors on your own body, then by George, violate all the rules and wear them every day of the week.

COLOR COMBOS
TESS LOVES TO WEAR:

- Baby pink and blue
- Fuchsia and neon green
- All black
- Lime green and electric blue
- Hot pink and cyan
- Peach and burnt orange
- Lavender and teal

I Need Clothes in My Size and Budget: Thrifting

What if you'd love to create new looks and experiment with styles, but your pockets are full of lint and, like, four dollars? Thrift stores got your back on this. Both Tess and Kelly shopped from thrift stores growing up and still do. Thrifting can be easy on your wallet, is better for the environment than buying fast fashion, and can introduce you to a whole wide world of styles you might never have considered because the clothes might not be current with whatever is on trend.

TIPS FOR GETTING THRIFTY

1. **HIT UP THE MEN'S SECTION FOR BIGGER SIZES.** Sometimes clothing in the women's section isn't as size-inclusive as it could be. *Eye roll* The good news? The men's section tends to carry bigger sizes. You never know when you'll find your next favorite grandpa sweater or flannel.

2. **HIT UP THE KIDS' SECTION FOR SMALLER SIZES.** Need to go down in size? Try the juniors or children's area. A boy's pair of XL basketball shorts can sometimes fit like a small or even medium in adult sizing, depending on the brand! You never know until you poke around.

3. **DON'T SKIP THE ACCESSORIES.** Aunt Agatha's donated costume jewelry? Yes, please. The accessories section is often flush with stuff that can get your brain going and inspire creativity in your outfits.

4. **UPCYCLE.** Use old clothes in new ways. Cut the legs off a pair of jeans to make shorts. Crop the bottom half of a baggy sweatshirt. Sew a patch onto an old bucket hat. Iron a quote onto the back of a jacket. Dye that white T-shirt. If you're able to sew, hit up the bedding section of the thrift store, and turn a handmade quilt into a sweater!

What If I Hate How I Look in Everything?

From Tess to You

Hate how you look? Congrats, that's totally normal. You're human. Everyone feels that way one time or another, even the people who seem the most confident. Recognizing that we're all in the same boat can help!

We get it. Your body might have recently changed or you might be growing in ways you didn't expect. You feel like you're not _____ enough. (Fill in that blank with whatever societal expectation you don't believe you're meeting right now.)

If you're trying on outfits and just cannot stand the way you look in anything because the Negativity Monster is chomping at your brain, we want you to repeat these four things to shut it up:

1. "It's the clothes, not my body. I need to find things that make me feel good."

2. "Even if I feel like it's my body, I'm growing and changing, and that's okay."

3. "I'm beautiful just the way I am, and every part of me is good."

4. "I'm allowed to wear what I like in the body I'm in right now."

The thing is, looking different from how you look right now or achieving some sort of physical milestone—being bigger, thinner, stronger, taller, curvier, shorter, etc.—will not change how you feel inside, even though you might think it's the key to happiness.

It isn't.

People tend to have a general happiness baseline—where they hang out on the sad-to-happy spectrum. The second we hit whatever physical milestone we think we need to achieve to finally be happy, we get a boost of excitement, which lasts for a couple of days. But then!!! We do this awful thing and *adapt* to our new normal. Boo! We settle back into our baseline happiness state, and then we have to hit a brand-new goal to get that little burst of excitement again.

It's a biting, vicious cycle that traps tons and tons of people into trying to change their bodies so they can be at peace with themselves. Ugh.

The good news? Science says that accepting yourself exactly as you are can *actually* boost your happiness. So can this stuff:

- Being compassionate
- Being humble and patient
- Letting go of grudges
- Choosing to live a life with meaning and purpose

A Final Word on Finding Your Fit

You're 100 percent worth having a meaningful life—one that gives you joy and hope and all the love you can possibly stand. You're 100 percent worth choosing clothes you love to live in and wearing them proudly in the body that you're living in today.

No exceptions. No compromises.

We promise.

QUIZ TIME

Who's Your Style Icon?

Answer each question, and keep track of the letters you choose.
Don't worry! We're not grading you.

1. **Which color combo speaks to you the most?**

   A. Lime green and electric blue

   B. All black

   C. Blush and burgundy

   D. Barbie pink and Tiffany blue

   E. Beige and cream

   F. Navy and orange

2. **Pick two adjectives that match your fashion vibe.**

   A. Wild and surprising

   B. Gothic and edgy

   C. Timeless and elegant

   D. Chic and trendy

   E. Urban and street inspired

   F. Athletic and comfortable

3. **Which statement is your go-to?**

   A. Better to be too much than too little.

   B. I am a shadow, where secrets whisper in the silence.

   C. In a world of disaster, be the polish and elegance it needs.

   D. I lead; others follow.

   E. I stay edgy and unpredictable.

   F. As long as it's got pockets, I'm in.

4. **Which silhouette do you tend to go for?**

   A. Anything goes—I love mixing it up!

   B. Form-fitting and tailored

   C. Structured and sophisticated

   D. Cropped and comfortable

   E. Oversized and unconventional

   F. Sporty and relaxed

5. **Which fabric is your ideal choice if you're trying to show up and show out?**

   A. Velvet and sequins

   B. Leather and lace

   C. Linen and silk

   D. Satin and organza

   E. Camouflage and denim

   F. Cotton and jersey

6. **How do you feel about embellishments and trimmings on your clothes?**

   A. The more, the merrier.

   B. Only if they're metal.

   C. Maybe one or two if they're subtle and classic.

   D. Yes, to glamorous and eye-catching stuff!

   E. I like a couple of unique pieces that make a statement.

   F. No. Just no.

7. Choose an accessory.

A. Stacked friendship bracelets
   (at least four)

B. Black oversized square sunglasses
   (so they know you mean business)

C. Small diamond stud earrings (passed down
   from your great-grandma)

D. Gold hoop earrings, nameplate necklaces
   (because you're THEM)

E. Your cell phone (to document your drip)

F. Headphones (because the game's on)

**8. Which pair of shoes are you grabbing
in the morning?**

A. Glitter or leather boots or trendy sneakers

B. Black Mary Janes, stilettos, Vans,
   or platform boots

C. Timeless and elegant flats or loafers

D. Platform slides, sandals,
   or cowboy boots

E. Combat boots or fashion sneakers

F. Athletic or running shoes

Answers

IF YOU CHOSE MOSTLY A'S: Get inspired by glam looks from Beyoncé, Harry Styles, Lil Nas X, Lizzo, Kacey Musgraves, or Taylor Swift on tour.

IF YOU CHOSE MOSTLY B'S: Go dark punk or metal with Olivia Rodrigo, Jenna Ortega as Wednesday Addams, Kylo Ren, Gwen Stefani, Willow Smith, or anyone from Metallica.

IF YOU CHOSE MOSTLY C'S: Get your elegant and timeless look by studying Idris Elba, Lupita Nyong'o, Audrey Hepburn, Zendaya, Mandy Moore, Munroe Bergdorf, or Penn Badgley.

IF YOU CHOSE MOSTLY D'S: Stay chic and trendy by looking to our very own Tess Holliday, along with Emma Chamberlain, Florence Pugh, Zoë Kravitz, Tyler the Creator, Tan France, or Bretman Rock.

IF YOU CHOSE MOSTLY E'S: Follow a more street style with looks from A$AP Rocky, Eminem, Billie Eilish, Rihanna, Pharrell Williams, Dylan Minnette, or Lana Condor on occasion.

IF YOU CHOSE MOSTLY F'S: Go sporty and casual with Justin Bieber, David Beckham, Jennifer Garner, Chris Hemsworth, Lewis Capaldi, or Michael B. Jordan.

Tess's Extras

Can't find something to wear? Here's Tess's list of
body-inclusive clothing brands for anyone and everyone:

- ASOS
- Dia & Co
- Eloquii
- Girlfriend
  Collective

- H&M
- Hot Topic
- Madewell
- Miaou
- ModCloth
- Selkie

- Skims
- Target
- Universal
  Standard
- WRAY

Find Your Fit Discussion
QUESTIONS

You'll find questions like these at the end of every chapter. *You're welcome*
😛 Use them to start convos with your friends, your neighbor with the good
pool, a whole classful of students you're mentoring, or even family members
at the next holiday gathering. (Listen. It's better than fielding endless questions about your dating life, and you know it.)

1. If you could design a fashion line inspired by a book, movie, or TV show,
what source would you use, and what would your clothes look like?
(Check out the last interview with Tess, on page 143, to read her answer
to this question!)

2. Pretend you went thrifting. When you touched an article of clothing, it
transported you back to the past, mid-conversation with its former owner.
What item of clothing did you touch, and whom did you meet?

3. If you could trade closets with anyone in the world for a day, whom
would you choose and why?

4. What outfit makes you feel the very best when you wear it?

5. Describe a time when you were forced to wear something you definitely
did not want to. What was the occasion? Why did it stress you out?

CHAPTER 2

ABOUT FACE

*T*OYA GREEN IS A SIXTEEN-YEAR-OLD LIVING HER BEST LIFE. SHE plays volleyball, leads her volunteer dog-walking group, and is earning an A in AP Seminar from one of the toughest teachers in school. She posts a picture of herself to her Snap stories and shoves her phone in her backpack, waiting for her teacher to quit yapping. During lunch she finds out that Lauren Johnson has screen-grabbed the photo, drawn an electric yellow circle around Toya's giant forehead pimple, and posted it to Instagram. Three hours later it's been shared hundreds of times. Someone even made an entire page called "Toya's Forehead Zit" and photoshopped her pimple onto pictures of every U.S. president since William Howard Taft.

Toya wants to crawl into a hole. Not only did she think she'd perfected her twelve-step skincare routine, but she didn't realize a pimple had cropped up in the middle of school and definitely didn't see it before she posted a picture. Now she has to move on with her day as if none of it bothers her because acting hurt puts a W in Lauren's column, and Toya's tired of losing.

Facing Your Face

Toya thinks about her face at least once an hour. Whenever she passes a mirror, she's wondering whether her cheeks are too shiny, her makeup too smeary, her forehead too pimply, or her eyes too puffy. She asks the mirror why she can't have the glowy skin that social media promised her with a money-back guarantee when she bought that miracle serum a month ago.

What a scam.

Do you ever feel like that? Determined to have a flawless complexion and S-T-R-E-S-S-E-D because it never happens? Dr. Nika Douvikas, our pediatrician consultant, says that although there isn't a miracle serum (despite that money-back guarantee), there are just three steps most teenagers need to take to care for their skin: cleansing, moisturizing, and applying sunscreen.

SKINCARE STEP 1:
ALL ABOUT THE SCREEN

We're sorry to be the bearers of bad news, but sunscreen is a must unless, when you're older, you (a) want to have a doctor surgically scrape skin cancer off your face, or (b) want to look like a grocery bag that's been bunched into a ball and smoothed back out.

Three Fast Facts About Sunscreen

1. **BROAD-SPECTRUM SUNSCREEN PROTECTS AGAINST UV RAYS:** Ultraviolet rays are the devil for your skin. They can damage you, burn you, and give ya skin cancer. Broad-spectrum sunscreen protects against both UVA rays, which go deeper into the skin, and also UVB rays that hit up the surface.

2. **THE SPF (SUN PROTECTION FACTOR) IS NOT RELATED TO TIME:** There's a myth going around that the number on the bottle correlates to the minutes you can hang out in the sun, but that was probably just started by a parent who was tired of reapplying sunscreen to their wriggly toddler. It's true that SPF 50 will protect you longer than SPF 8, but how long is affected by things like a person's melanin, the time of day, and where you're sitting on the globe.

3. **YOU NEED TO APPLY SUNSCREEN OFTEN AND SLATHER IT ON:** The more sunscreen you wear, the fewer UV rays you absorb. Also? You *must* reapply because sunscreen wears off.

Hate your forehead feeling greasy? Try one of these SPF products designed specifically for your face:

- Supergoop Unseen Sunscreen (SPF 40)
- Colorescience Sunforgettable Brush-on Powder (SPF 50)
- EltaMD UV Clear Face Sunscreen, clear or tinted (SPF 46)
- Neutrogena Sheer Zinc Dry-Touch Face Sunscreen (SPF 50)

SKINCARE STEPS 2 & 3:
CLEANSER AND MOISTURIZER

You might need a different cleanser and moisturizer depending on whether your skin is dry, sensitive, oily, or acne prone. Dermatologists who specialize in this kind of stuff recommend those in the table here, and you can find them without a prescription too:

SKIN TYPE	CLEANSER	MOISTURIZER
DRY Choose products with moisturizing ingredients like ceramides and hyaluronic acid.	CeraVe Hydrating Facial Cleanser	CeraVe Moisturizing Cream or Neutrogena Hydro Boost Face Moisturizer
ACNE PRONE Choose deep cleansers with benzoyl peroxide or salicylic acid and great moisturizers to combat the drying effects of the cleansers.	CeraVe Acne Foaming Cream Cleanser or Neutrogena Oil-Free Acne Wash Pink Grapefruit Facial Cleanser	Neutrogena Hydro Boost Face Moisturizer
OILY Choose cleansers with hydrating ceramides and niacinamide, an ingredient that tamps down inflammation, and moisturizers labeled noncomedogenic that won't clog pores.	La Roche-Posay Toleriane Hydrating Gentle Face Cleanser	CeraVe AM Facial Moisturizing Lotion with SPF 30
SENSITIVE Choose gentle products with glycerin, vitamins like panthenol (B-5), oat extract, and niacinamide to soothe irritation.	Cetaphil Face Wash Hydrating Gentle Skin Cleanser for Dry to Normal Sensitive Skin	Aveeno Calm + Restore Oat Gel Facial Moisturizer for Sensitive Skin

THE ACNE AMONG US

Acne—including whiteheads, blackheads, and cysts—can be a gigantic pain in the yee-haw for a lot of teens. They can show up for different reasons too, says Dr. Douvikas. One of them is hormones. They go bonkers during adolescence and produce a ton of oil, so when a pore gets blocked with dead skin or dirt, the extra oil can't escape and—*voila!*—a pimple pops up like an ugly little rabbit from a hat.

What can you do about it? Well, it depends. According to the American Academy of Dermatology, you should ask yourself these questions to figure out whether a dermatology visit is in your near future:

1. Have you tried to treat your acne, but it doesn't go away?

2. Did your acne start between the ages of eight and eleven?

3. Do you have acne in unusual spots like your armpits, backs of your upper arms, or thighs?

4. Is your acne deep and painful?

5. Do you feel anxious or depressed about your acne?

If you answered yes to any of these, then Dr. Douvikas recommends calling a doctor. If your breakouts are more of the typical type and you want to do something about a forehead blemish that rears its ugly head in the middle of your AP Seminar class, then consider these options:

1. IF YOU WANT TO TREAT IT:

- Use spot creams like Differin Acne Treatment Gel or Sunday Riley Saturn Sulfur and Niacinamide Acne Spot Treatment Mask (Tess's fav!) to dry it out. Dr. Douvikas also recommends adapalene gel and La Roche-Posay, which are over-the-counter topical retinoids. If you start using this stuff, talk to your pediatrician so they can give you tips and maybe even refer you to a pediatric dermatologist to figure out if other acne treatments are a good match for you.
- Try pimple patches like Hero Cosmetics Mighty Patch Original Patch Hydrocolloid Acne Pimple Patches or Peace Out Skincare Acne Dots Hydrocolloid Pimple Patches to cover it up and heal it.

2. IF YOU WANT TO HIDE IT:

- Choose concealers like e.l.f. Hydrating Camo Concealer or L'Oreal Paris Infallible Full Wear Waterproof Matte Concealer. Dab a little bit on a clean finger or makeup sponge, and blend carefully. Finish with powder to set it all day.
- Use a brown or black eyeliner to turn it into a freckle or mini-mole. Cutest cute!
- Wear stickers like Starface Hydro-Stars Party Pack to cover it up with a little flair. Who said you have to blend in?

3. IF YOU WANT TO EMBRACE IT:

- Draw a heart around it with a fun eyeliner color.
- Dab some glitter on it.
- Just wash your face knowing that zits happen to the best of us.

That's a Lovely 'Stache You Have

Facial hair is funny. Some people are staring in the mirror, willing chin hairs to grow right this very second, while others are wishing their chin hairs would disappear into the void forever.

Facial hair exists for nearly everyone in various lengths, thicknesses, colors, textures, and locations, and we might as well just accept that this is universal so we can focus on other things like when Netflix is going to premier a new reality dating show. (It's been months!)

WHAT'S WITH FACIAL HAIR?

Typically, genetic males can grow facial hair because their follicles get activated during puberty by the hormone dihydrotestosterone (DHT), which comes from testosterone (T). And while genetic females have the same number of follicles, they tend to have less testosterone, so they're usually less affected by DHT.

Facial hair often follows a growth pattern too. Mustaches sprout first, followed by sideburns, chin hair, and, finally, those cheek whiskers. Your genetics and hormones play a huge role in how much facial hair you get, which explains why some fifth-graders are sporting majestic mustaches while others don't have a single whisker until they're eighteen.

> ### HAIRLESS DOESN'T NECESSARILY MEAN BETTER
>
> There's no moral high ground in having a hairless face. While many of us chop down or yank out as much facial hair as we possibly can, others sport it in all of its glory, and both ways of handling it are perfectly reasonable. It's your own dang face. Do what makes you happy.

I'M A GIRL WITH FACIAL HAIR. HELP.

Don't stress. There are *plenty* of us with mustaches, sideburns, chin sprouts, and even full beards. We're mammals. We all grow hair. Some girls grow more than others because of genetics and conditions like polycystic ovary syndrome (PCOS), Cushing syndrome, congenital adrenal hyperplasia, tumors, and even medication. Trust us when we say there are more women waxing, plucking, shaving, depilating, and threading their faces than you can even imagine. With that being said, if you have more hair on your body than average—especially on your back, chin, or back of the neck, for example—then talk to your doctor, because a treatable condition might be causing it.

GROOMING FACIAL HAIR

You've got it and you want to take care of it:

• **WASH IT.** Yes, even that scraggly little mustache needs a cleaning. Your hair sits on top of your skin, and if you don't scrub daily, all that oil and dead skin can cause blemishes to pop up.

• **TRIM IT.** Grab a fine-tooth comb and a pair of small, curved scissors. Tweezerman sells brow-shaping scissors that are perfect for this sort of thing. Comb, then hack it off.

- **SMOOTH IT.** You don't need to use grooming products, but if you want your facial hair to hold a particular shape, a little beard balm or wax can turn your sideburns into Wolverine's or give you a villainous mustache to twirl.

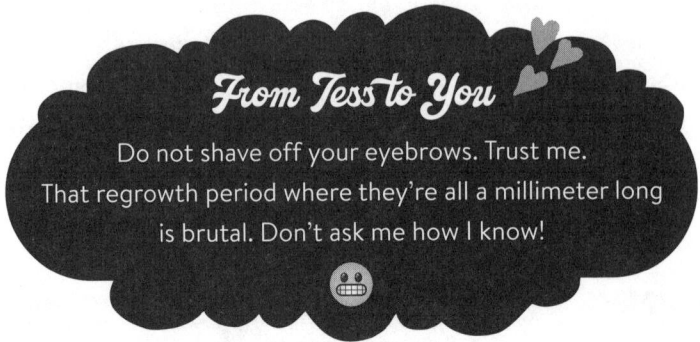

From Tess to You

Do not shave off your eyebrows. Trust me.
That regrowth period where they're all a millimeter long
is brutal. Don't ask me how I know!

REMOVING FACIAL HAIR

You've got it and you want to get rid of it:

- **SHAVE IT.** With a regular safety razor, dermaplaning tool, or electric razor, it's easy enough to cut the hair at the skin level. This means you'll probably need to do it again the next day, but it does *not* mean that it will grow back thicker and darker. (Yet another myth!)
- **PULL IT.** By threading, waxing, or epilating with a specific tool for the face, you can yank the hair out at the roots, delaying when you'll want to remove it again. Sidenote: *Ouch!*
- **DISSOLVE IT.** Hair removal creams use thioglycolic acid to break down keratin that turns the hair into a pile of mush you can wipe away. The good news? It's not painful like pulling it out by the root. The bad news? Sensitive skin can get irritated, and it doesn't last as long as pulling.
- **ZAP IT.** Lasers are often pricey, but they can zap the hair follicle, which will make the hair grow back more slowly. It only works on dark hair, though, because melanin absorbs the laser light—no melanin, no zappy. It's also most effective on people with light skin.

Let's Make Up

First, let's get something straight: makeup is for anyone who wants to wear it. Period. End of sentence. Throughout history people have worn makeup in hundreds of cultures across the globe. Today people wear makeup for as many reasons as there are grains of sand on every Florida beach. Makeup can showcase spectacular cheekbones. Highlight a favorite feature. Hide an irritating birthmark, mole, scar, or pimple. Turn you into Hellboy. Whatever gets you outta bed in the morning.

While we stan a natural face as much as we support the right to contour your nose into the shape of a Christmas tree, our goal is to offer you a few pointers in case you *do* want to dabble in some color.

MAKEUP TIPS

1. **START WITH THE SKIN.** It's vital that your face is clean, moisturized, and protected from the sun before you go elbows deep in an eyeshadow palette. Clean skin = fewer breakouts, less bacteria, and the removal of pizza sauce from the corner of your mouth.

2. **COLOR MATCH.** If you're not sure what color concealer or foundation to get, head to a cosmetics counter at the mall, Ulta, Sephora, or similar. Ask to be color matched. They'll likely try different bases along your jawline to make sure that the color is a perfect blend between your face and neck.

3. **WASH YOUR TOOLS.** Dirty makeup brushes, sponges, and applicators can cause infections, which can be very serious! To protect your skin, wash your tools every seven to ten days with a gentle shampoo, face wash, or soap for that express purpose. Clean them until the water runs clear, then lay them on a towel to dry. Replace sponges every two to three months, and for the love of Pete, don't share your tools, even if your bestie asks you very nicely. Eye infections are *not* fun.

OOOH, TRY THESE LEWKS

Since you can find a thousand different ways to paint your face on YouTube, we'll keep this short. (Otherwise, you'll still be reading this book to your grand-kids fifty years from now.) Here are a few of our faves:

	FOR SCHOOL	FOR A NIGHT OUT	FOR PROM
SKIN	• Tinted sunscreen • Concealer under eyes and on forehead	• Concealer under eyes and on forehead • Highlight the tip of the nose, above the lip, and middle of chin	• Foundation to match neck • Concealer under eyes and on forehead • Highlight the tip of the nose, above the lip, and middle of chin
EYES	• Curl lashes • A light coating of clear or colored mascara or Aquaphor on a spoolie, and curl again	• Curl lashes • Mascara • A dusting of eyeshadow in a neutral color	• Curl lashes • Black mascara or apply lashes • Light color under brows • Darker color in the crease and on outside part of lid • Shimmer, glitter, or rhinestones in the inner corner of eye and inner lid—whatever makes you feel beautiful • Eyeliner along upper lash line
BROWS	• Comb	• Brow gel or pencil in sparse spots	• Brow gel or pencil in sparse spots
CHEEKS	• Concealer on any blemishes	• Cream blush on apples of cheeks	• Contour under cheekbones and blend • Bronzer on cheeks • Blush on cheekbones • Light highlight above blush
LIPS	• Gloss or tinted lip balm	• Light lipstick or lip stain	• Bold lipliner • Bold plumping lipstick or lip stain to last all night

From Tess to You

Can't do a winged eyeliner to save your life? Stick a piece of Scotch tape under the outside corner of your eye, angled toward the tail of your brow. Dab a small brush into dark eyeshadow. Starting about one-fourth of the way up the tape, drag the color down toward your eye, along the tape's edge to the lash line. Then drag it along the lash line to the middle of your eyelid. Blend and remove the tape. If you want a crispier line, use an eyeliner pencil. Don't move on to a liquid liner until you've conquered both the shadow and the pencil.

Strike a Pose

We couldn't end this chapter without addressing the giant, trumpeting elephant in the room, which is that many of us are nervous about the photos we (and Toya's nemesis Lauren) post online.

Rule of thumb: When posting pics of others . . . don't. Unless, of course, you have their permission. When posting pics of yourself, consider using some modeling tricks to showcase that gorgeous face of yours.

TESS'S TRICKS FOR JUST THE RIGHT SHOT:

- **FIND YOUR LIGHT.** Depending on where you position yourself related to sunshine, you can create different looks. Put the light directly in front of you to bring out all the details. Light falling on the side of your face from a window creates softer edges. And if you want to look like a dewy angel, put the light behind you so you glow.
- **PLAY WITH ANGLES.** If you're worried about the shape of your face, act like you have a string tied to the top of your head that pulls you taller. It elongates your neck. You can also stick your tongue to the roof of your mouth, point your chin toward the camera, and tilt your head. A head tilt to the right is Tess's go-to!
- **TRY FOCUSING ON A DIFFERENT FEATURE.** If you want a natural pursed lip, breathe out gently. If you want your eyes to sparkle, think of someone you love or something exciting, like smashing a homerun over the fence.
- **TAKE UP SPACE.** Keep your shoulders back and hold your head high. Tall people don't need to hunch to take pics with short people. Big people don't need to squeeze to the side for smaller people. Take up all the space you need!
- **IT'S NOT THAT SERIOUS.** Taking pictures isn't brain surgery. You won't die or take out anyone else if you make the wrong move, so take a deep breath before you pull out your phone. Make like a cat lady's living room and live, laugh, love. Have fun, even! We dare you. =)

A Final Word About Your Face

You know what? We love your face. And we're betting there are people in your life who love your face too, even if they've never said it. Your nose is cute. Your eyes are a delight. And don't even get us started on your smile. We want you to look in the mirror or in your phone's camera *right now* and repeat this phrase at least ten times every day or until you believe it, whichever comes first: "I'm stunning, I radiate light, and I am perfectly content with who I am."

QUIZ TIME

Which Face Are You Showing the World?

Answer each question, and keep track of the letters you choose.
This time it's for a grade. JOKES. Jokes.

1. How do you prep your face for the day?

A. Wake up, wash my face, maybe shave or maybe not, and apply SPF if I'm feeling responsible.

B. Wash, moisturize, and brush on some light makeup to highlight my features.

C. Full skincare routine. Full glam makeup.

D. Embrace my natural self. Take a shower and head out the door.

2. How do you manage unwanted facial hair?

A. Regularly remove it when it starts to get wild.

B. Light grooming to maintain a clean look.

C. Tweeze, wax, shave, or thread.

D. No grooming required!

3. What's your typical choice for eye makeup?

A. I might swipe on some mascara or not, depending on the day.

B. A subtle eyeshadow look to enhance my eyes.

C. Full-on shading and dramatic lashes.

D. Au naturel—I let my eyes shine on their own.

4. How about your cheeks?

A. I've dabbed concealer on a zit before.

B. Some bronzer to define my cheekbones.

C. Contouring, bronzer, blush, and highlight to sculpt and define my face.

D. What about them?

5. Lip game, strong or subtle?

A. Just lip balm if my lips are crusty.

B. A natural lip color with a touch of gloss.

C. Bold lipstick or lip plumping for a statement pout.

D. Keep it simple—I let my lips speak for themselves (get it?).

6. You wake up with a blemish on your face. What's your reaction?

A. Apply targeted acne treatment immediately.

B. Treat it, then conceal it with makeup and continue my day.

C. Treat it and cover it up with heavy makeup—no one will know!

D. Accept it as part of life—no treatment, no worries.

7. Your daily skincare routine is best described as:

A. Minimal, focusing on my own looks without many products

B. Balanced, with a few key products for a healthy glow

C. Elaborate, involving many products for a perfect canvas

D. Nonexistent

8. How often do you go makeup-free?

A. Almost daily except when I need to cover up a pimple or two.

B. Occasionally, on weekends or casual days.

C. Almost never—makeup is my daily routine.

D. Daily unless it's Halloween.

9. How often do you groom your eyebrows?

A. Sometimes

B. Often

C. Regularly

D. Rarely

10. At the end of the day you take care of your face by:

A. Taking a shower if I've been active.

B. Using a makeup wipe to get rid of any makeup and applying moisturizer.

C. Scrubbing my face, wearing a mask, moisturizing, applying a serum, and dabbing on eye cream.

D. Falling face-first into my pillow.

Answers

IF YOU CHOSE MOSTLY A'S: You're fresh-faced and decent with SPF, though you could probably use it more regularly. Keep up the skincare routine to make sure you're not advancing your risk for certain skin cancers.

IF YOU CHOSE MOSTLY B'S: You're effortlessly polished. You take care of your skin and present a freshly made-up face to the world. Consider trying a green swap for your makeup remover wipes with a cleanser and washcloth.

IF YOU CHOSE MOSTLY C'S: You're glamorous and ready to conquer the day with your skincare and makeup routine. Talk to a dermatologist if your products are taking a toll on your skin. Too many with harsh ingredients can cause sensitive skin to flare up.

IF YOU CHOSE MOSTLY D'S: You're natural and prefer the least fuss as is possible. Give washing your face at the beginning and end of the day a try. Follow the morning clean-up with a moisturizer and an SPF lotion to keep your skin healthy.

Draw It Out

Time to doodle! Get out some markers or crayons and a pencil.
Get a sheet of paper and fold it into four equal sections.

IN SECTION ONE, draw an object that represents the person who sees you for who you really are. Maybe a cupcake or a football for your best friend or a cozy sweater for someone else you love.

IN SECTION TWO, draw an object that represents how confident you feel when you're with them. Maybe it's a mountain or a roller coaster.

IN SECTION THREE, draw an object that represents how you feel when you haven't seen them in a while. Maybe a storm cloud, a melting candle, or a broken heart.

IN SECTION FOUR, write their name and decorate it.

If you're really feeling what you end up with, give your drawing to the person who makes you feel that good.

About Face Discussion
QUESTIONS

1. Which celebrity has the best facial hair? The best smile?

2. In the past, men would be ridiculed for using facial skincare products. What shifted in our world to make it acceptable for men to be concerned about their skin?

3. Imagine you could swap facial features with someone you know for a day. Name three reasons you'd choose them.

4. On a scale of 1 to 5, with 1 being never and 5 being constantly, how much do you think about what your face looks like in a typical day? How comfortable are you with that number?

5. What's one facial feature you get compliments on? Which one do you *wish* you'd get compliments on?

CHAPTER 3

DOING THE DO

KELLY: What's the craziest thing you've ever done to your hair?

TESS: I have way too many stories. Do you want trauma or—

KELLY: Let's go light, haha! But don't you worry. We'll make sure we poke around for other extremely tragic and dramatic stories for other chapters.

TESS: Great. Can't wait. Haha! Wanna hear about the time I dressed up like Cruella de Vil?

KELLY: I mean, absolutely? Is there ever a time I'd say no to that? Anything villainous is a yes.

TESS: Okay, you will love this. Sooooo one time, when I was a teenager, I wanted to be Cruella de Vil for Halloween. But instead of buying a wig like a normal person, I bleached the right half of my head and dyed the other half black.

KELLY: That's commitment to the bit.

TESS: Yeah, but note to self: you cannot bleach your head three times in one day because when you try to brush your hair later, massive clumps will be stuck in the bristles.

KELLY: I'm sorry, but *MASSIVE CLUMPS*?

TESS: The whole front right side of my hair *fell out*, Kelly. It fell out.

KELLY: Oh noooooooooooo! What did you *do*?

TESS: Well, I worked at Hot Topic at the time, so I just combed it over.

KELLY: You *combed it over*? HAHAHAHAHA

TESS: Hahahahahaha, I know! I know. I wish I'd taken pictures.

KELLY: I mean, that's remarkable resilience though.

TESS: What else could I do? I got on with life, half-bald. Dazzling.

KELLY: Oh my gosh, Tess. You're a legend. This is iconic.

TESS: Told ya you'd like it. Moral of the story: Never do that, though. NEVER. Do you hear that, readers? Leave the bleach to the professionals.

The Hair Sprouting from Your Skull

Maybe you've got hair trouble. Perhaps, like Tess, you've done something—er—extra to your hair or gotten a haircut you regretted because it made you look like Sonic the Hedgehog. Maybe dandruff is your nemesis and you're over it. This chapter is here to help! Whether you're solving a hair issue, curious about trying a new hairstyle, or simply wondering how much is *too* much shampoo, you're in the right spot.

What's My Type?

Celebrity stylist Andre Walker was the first person to put together a modern hair-typing system, which assigned numbers to different types: 1 = straight, 2 = wavy, 3 = curly, and 4 = kinky. He debuted the system on *The Oprah Winfrey Show* in the 1990s because he'd developed products to care for each type of hair and figured the system would help people know which ones to buy. Since then people have added subcategories, and now hair-typing charts look a little something like this:

Hair-Typing System

TYPE 1	TYPE 2	TYPE 3	TYPE 4
Straight Hair	Wavy Hair	Curly Hair	Kinky Hair
Fine and fragile to coarse and thin (curl resistant)	Fine and thin to coarse and frizzy	Loose curls to corkscrew curls	Tight coils to Z-angled coils
A ———————	A ∿∿∿	A 𝒬𝒬𝒬𝒬	A ∿∿∿∿∿∿
B ———————	B ∿∿∿	B 𝒬𝒬𝒬𝒬𝒬	B ∿∿∿∿∿
C ———————	C ∿∿∿	C 𝒬𝒬𝒬𝒬𝒬	C ∿∿∿∿∿

It's More Than 1 to 4

A hair-typing system isn't enough to care for your hair, though. First, you can have more than one type. Tess is walking around with 3A and 2C strands. Second, the chart doesn't account for *all* types. We know half a dozen people who don't fit anywhere on this chart. Third, it doesn't show ya other stuff that's important to haircare, like the following:

1. **POROSITY:** How well your hair holds moisture.

- **Low porosity:** Hair products don't absorb well and water doesn't saturate the hair easily.
- **Medium porosity:** Hair holds styles easily, takes color well, and tends to look healthy.
- **High porosity:** Water and other moisturizing products are quickly absorbed and hair breaks easily, tends to be frizzy and dry, and dries quickly.

2. **ELASTICITY:** How stretchy your hair is.

- **Low elasticity:** Hair snaps immediately when stretched.
- **Medium elasticity:** Hair stretches partially before breaking.
- **High elasticity:** Hair stretches a long way before breaking.

3. **DENSITY:** How tightly strands are packed together on your head.

- **Low density:** You can easily see your scalp between strands.
- **Medium density:** You can partly see your scalp between strands.
- **High density:** You can't really see your scalp between strands.

4. **TEXTURE:** How wide a single strand is compared to a piece of thread.

- **Fine texture:** Thinner than the thread, lacks volume, and can be weighed down by products.

- **Medium texture:** About the same as a strand of thread, less likely to break than fine hair, and holds styles well.
- **Coarse texture:** Thicker than thread, and gives your hair high volume.

Scrubbing Up

You can have any combination of all that stuff too. For example, your hair could have high porosity, medium elasticity, low density, and a coarse texture. Or low porosity, high elasticity, high density, and fine texture. And caring for either of those hair types the same way would give you wildly different results.

Some people wash their hair daily and that works for them, while others who wear protective styles might suds up a couple of times a month. So how do you know how often to wash *your* hair? Should you use conditioner? A leave-in conditioner? GAH. It's a lot. We know. Tym Wallace, our celebrity hair-care expert, is here to save the day. He recommends these guidelines to care for your hair, no matter your type, but he says lots of things factor into hair-care. It's best to try things out and see what works for you.

HAIR TYPE	CLEANSERS	CONDITIONERS
1 and 2	Use a lightweight shampoo that gently cleanses the hair approximately 3-4 times per week.	Use a conditioner that isn't too heavy so it doesn't weigh the hair down after you cleanse.
Tym's types 1 and 2 recommended products	TPH by Taraji Hustle & Co or Serene Queen Shampoo	TPH by Taraji Make it Rain Conditioner
3	Use a clarifying and moisturizing shampoo approximately two times per week.	Use moisturizing conditioners and/or leave-in conditioners after you cleanse.
Tym's type 3 recommended products	TPH by Taraji Honey Fresh Shampoo	TPH by Taraji Ride or Die Leave-in Conditioner
4	Use a moisturizing shampoo that's really concentrated to hydrate the hair approximately once a week.	Use leave-in conditioner to hydrate the hair.
Tym's type 4 recommended products	It's a 10 Miracle Coily Hydrating Shampoo or TPH by Taraji So Lengthy Shampoo	TPH by Taraji New Levelz Strengthening & Lengthening Conditioner and Mask On Conditioning Hair Mask

I Need a New Look STAT

It's weird when you go from being a little kid to a teen, right? Suddenly you have this irresistible urge to go rogue with your hair. This can make the adults in your life grumpy, but we know for a fact they'll get over it.

If you want a more permanent change:

- **PERMS:** Whether you want to go from curly to straight or straight to curly, perms can make it happen. The chemical solution breaks the hair's disulfide bond, and then fixative remakes the bond in the new position. A heads-up: some people might have reactions to this process, and your hair will be stuck in this new shape until it grows out or you cut it off.

- **DYEING:** Permanent dye is a little bit of a lie. Obviously your hair grows and the new hair won't be dyed, so it's not like you're committing to a lifetime of florescent pink if you went there. It does last a lot longer than a glaze or a gloss, though, because ammonia and hydrogen peroxide open the hair cuticle and change the structure. When your hair grows, your roots near your scalp will contrast with the new color.

ICONIC CELEBRITY HAIRSTYLES:

- Jennifer Aniston's The Rachel
- Zoë Kravitz's pixie cut
- Justin Bieber's swoopy bangs
- The Weeknd's freeform locs
- Bob Ross's curly perm

If commitment isn't your thing:

- **HAIRCUTS:** Healthy hair grows about a half-inch a month on average. If you lop off two inches, you'll be back to where you were in less time than it takes to master the ACT science section.

- **SEMI-PERMANENT DYEING:** If, unlike Tess, you're *not* committed to a bit, you could try a glaze or gloss. These semi-permanent hair colors stain the hair for three to six washes. You can also go demi-permanent, which is dye that lasts for about twenty-five shampoos. Either way, they won't leave a lasting impact like, you know, BLEACH.

- **KERATIN TREATMENTS:** This is when a stylist applies a coating of protein to your hair to help you manage the frizz. It can last about three months, but there is some controversy about using it. Some treatments release formaldehyde, a gas that can cause allergic reactions and sometimes even cancer. Ask the stylist and a trusted adult before having this treatment!

- **WIGS:** A wig can be a great way to experiment. There's no commitment, and you can take it off if you hate it.
- **HAIRPIECES:** Want more hair but not an entire wig? Hairpieces, like extensions, can be clipped or sewn in to your actual hair to add fullness or length. If you've lost some of your hair but don't want to wear a wig, some hairpieces can be glued directly onto the scalp!
- **STYLING:** Go ahead. Try cornrows instead of the box braids you usually wear. Start flat ironing your hair straight instead of letting your beachy waves fly. Part it to the side. Slick it back with gel. Pick out a natural afro. Tie it back into a low ponytail, or add fourteen butterfly clips (we won't tell 1998 what you did).

From Tess to You

Don't be afraid to experiment with your style. My hairstylist Angelina Panelli has given me all sorts of looks over the years—space buns, long pigtail braids, sleek buns, bouncy natural curls, and seventy-five other styles. Try different things to see what *you* like. Trust yourself!

I've Got Hair Issues

When Tess was around fourteen she was arguing with her little brother, Tad. They got to the threat portion of the argument, which, if you don't have siblings, involves saying ridiculous things you're going to do to them if they don't obey you. Mostly, these threats never pan out.

So when Tad threatened to light Tess's hair on fire, Tess didn't believe him. However, he got up, grabbed a lit candle, and pretended to make good on his threat, holding it near her head. He didn't realize that Tess's hair was coated in hairspray, so *whoomp* up her head went in smoke.

Luckily they got the fire out quickly enough with no damage to person or location. But lesson learned. Hair products can be flammable and twelve-year-old brothers are not to be trusted. If you have hair issues unrelated to fire, check out Mr. Wallace's tips for handling them:

- **DANDRUFF:** If you have a healthy scalp, you have healthy, nonflaky hair, he says. He recommends the TPH scalp care system by Taraji P. Henson.

- **MATTING:** Sometimes you *want* your hair to mat, like when you're starting locs, but if you're just dealing with common tangles, get the Wet brush.
- **LICE:** Sometimes lice happens. It doesn't mean you're dirty. It means your head was close to someone else's head that had the little critters in there. Mr. Wallace says to use a medicated shampoo like NIX Lice Killing Crème Rinse and a nit comb to get those suckers out.

The Dos and Don'ts of Hair Etiquette

Hair issues can sometimes invite unwanted attention. Even when there *aren't* hair issues, you can get comments and even unwanted physical contact because of the way you wear your tresses. But, just like with other parts of your body, there are dos and don'ts when it comes to talking about or interacting with other people's hair.

DO	DON'T
Give compliments! "Your hair looks really great, Hassan." "I love your new curls!" "That color is perfect on you."	Give backhanded compliments. "Your hair *finally* looks really great, Hassan." "The curls are such an improvement." "I liked your natural color better, but this one's pretty good too."
Ask questions about a good friend's hairstyle. "I like those braids. What's that style called?"	Touch someone's hair—even a friend's—without their permission. It can make people feel like they're a sideshow or something exotic to be gawked at. No touchy.
Be curious about a stranger's hairstyle from afar. If you have questions, Google exists!	Ask a stranger about their hair. It can feel rude, nosy, intrusive, or simply exhausting, especially if nine other people asked about their hair today too.
Share hair care or style advice when someone asks you for it.	Tell people what to do with their own hair.
Quietly give someone a heads-up if you notice a *minor* problem with someone's hair that they can fix quickly (someone put gum in it, they have an extension falling out, etc.).	Embarrass someone by pointing out a minor hair issue in front of others. Before telling them at all, ask yourself whether it would make their day better or worse if they knew.
Tell a trusted adult when you notice a *major* problem with someone's hair (lice, unintentional matting, etc.).	Approach the person about a major hair problem. They could have things going on you don't need to know about.

**FOUR THINGS TO SAY
WHEN SOMEONE TOUCHES YOUR HAIR**

If someone touches your hair without permission, try these phrases (ranging from statements you can make to a friend or to someone harassing you):

1. I know you're just curious, but it feels really weird when you touch my hair. Next time ask, okay?

2. Please don't touch any part of me without asking, including my hair. Thank you!

3. Don't touch my hair.

4. I'm not a dog you can pet. Keep your hands off me.

A Final Word on Doing Your Do

We know that caring for your hair and trying new styles isn't like world-crisis-level stuff for some of you, but hair can be super important to others for *so* many reasons:

• It can be tied to your identity.

• It can make you feel like your world is collapsing if you have a hair problem you can't solve alone.

• It can make you feel left out, singled out, or lonely.

• It can make you feel proud if your particular hair type is celebrated.

But no matter whether your hair is something you love, hate, or feel pretty neutral about, Mr. Wallace says, "Know that we are all beautifully flawed. The Creator has made us the way we are, and God makes no mistakes."

Before we say goodbye to this hair chapter once and for all, we want to give you a little info about nails because of their cousin connection.

The Hair-Nail Connection

Hair and nails (and skin) are part of the outer layer of the body called the integumentary system and contain a protein called keratin. (No, you can't dye your nails like you can your hair, which is a real shame because manicures can be pricey.) Nails do, however, share some similarities, like requiring regular trims and annoying the heck out of you when you're trying to style them in a hurry.

Nail Care 101

- **KEEP THEM DRY AND CLEAN.** Use a little scrub brush or sterilized toothbrush to get under the edges.

- **USE MOISTURIZER ON THE NAIL AND CUTICLE TOO.** When you're moisturizing your hands, your nails want some love too! Don't ignore them—they're family!

- **CLIP OR FILE THEM STRAIGHT ACROSS AND GENTLY ROUND THE EDGES IF YOU WEAR SHORT NAILS.** Fair warning: you might get used to the ease of short nails if you do.

- **IF YOU WEAR ACRYLICS, GELS, DIPS, OR PRESS-ON NAILS, TAKE A BREAK BETWEEN MANICURES.** Sigh. We know. This one's hard. But it can help your nails stay strong if you're not constantly getting the top layer buzzed off every other week.

- **TRY NOT TO BITE OR PICK THEM.** Bacteria can crawl into the tiniest little breaks in the skin and wreak havoc. Nobody wants that.

- **FOR TOENAILS, KEEP THEM CLIPPED STRAIGHT ACROSS.** Unless you *like* the pain of an ingrown toenail (and if you've never had one, consider yourself lucky), don't file them to the shape of your toe. Keep them straight across to prevent them from digging in at the sides.

Got it? Great. Now go take the hairstyle quiz!

QUIZ TIME

Which Hairstyle Should You Try Next?

Answer each question and
keep track of the letters you choose.

1. Pick a band or musician:

A. Dua Lipa

B. Kendrick Lamar

C. Zac Brown Band

D. BTS

E. Taylor Swift

2. Which fruit would you eat for breakfast?

A. Avocado

B. Dragon fruit

C. Banana

D. Gala apple

E. Pineapple

3. What's the best piece of furniture in the house?

A. An elegant chaise lounge

B. A beanbag chair

C. A vintage record player

D. A minimalist bookshelf

E. A colorful gaming chair

4. Your next binge series genre is:

A. Classic romance

B. Sci-fi fantasy

C. Indie comedy

D. Thriller

E. Anime

5. Where are you going on vacay?

A. Paris, France

B. Tokyo, Japan

C. Bali, Indonesia

D. Zurich, Switzerland

E. Rio de Janeiro, Brazil

6. You need to MOVE. What are you doing?

A. Pilates

B. Mountain biking

C. Yoga

D. Weightlifting

E. Zumba

7. The social media platform you're posting your thoughts on:

A. I'm not

B. TikTok

C. Threads

D. Instagram

E. Snapchat

8. Pick a color for your bedroom rug:

A. Ivory

B. Midnight blue

C. Sage green

D. Charcoal gray

E. Sunshine yellow

9. What are you doing this weekend?

A. Visiting an art gallery

B. Hitting up a concert

C. Hiking, of course

D. Getting spruced up with a haircut
or spa day

E. Having a picnic!

10. Your pet, Lulu, is a:

A. Persian cat

B. Snake

C. Golden Retriever

D. Betta fish

E. Parrot

Answers

IF YOU CHOSE MOSTLY A'S: Try a sleek, high ponytail or slicked-back taper.

IF YOU CHOSE MOSTLY B'S: Embrace protective locs or a modern mohawk.

IF YOU CHOSE MOSTLY C'S: Go for effortless, tousled curls or waves.

IF YOU CHOSE MOSTLY D'S: Opt for a tight fade or chin-length bob.

IF YOU CHOSE MOSTLY E'S: Choose braids, a messy bun, or long, shaggy fringe.

Tess's Extras

Tess's Tricks for Keeping Your Hairstyle Looking Fresh

1. **DON'T MESS WITH YOUR HAIR ONCE IT'S STYLED.** The more you touch a blow-out, silk press, or any other style, the more you risk unstyling it. Let it do its thing!

2. **KEEP IT SNATCHED.** Use a light mist of hairspray, spritz, or hair oil to smooth strays. A spoolie and gel can help tame edges.

3. **USE DRY SHAMPOO.** Whether you sprinkle the powder in before styling or use it to refresh your hair a few days out, it can reshape and hold a look for hours.

4. **WORK WITH YOUR NATURAL OILS.** Don't have time to shampoo? If you have longer hair, pull it back into a sleek, high ponytail. If your hair's short, go for the fifties greaser look by parting and combing it. Set with hairspray.

5. **TRY FUN HAIR ACCESSORIES.** Pull long hair up into a French twist with a claw clip. Style curls around your face to keep it sweet, or pull some spiky pieces out of the top for a nineties retro look.

6. **GO OLD SCHOOL.** Keep bobby pins on you to pull back bangs or loose strands from an up-do. Remember to keep the bumpy side against your head and the flat side up.

Doing the Do Discussion

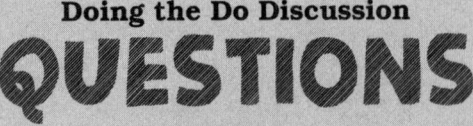

QUESTIONS

1. If hair can be a big part of your identity, how do you feel about schools regulating it?
2. Name two musicians with enviable hairstyles. What do you like about them?
3. Which hair trend from the past should stay in the past?
4. What do you think people assume about you based on your hair? If they're wrong, why are they?
5. What's your favorite shampoo? Why do you love it?

CHAPTER 4

FEED ME

FOOD CAN BE COMPLICATED, RIGHT? LOADS OF PEOPLE TELL you different things about what you should eat, when you should eat, how you should eat, why you should eat, and whom you should eat it with. Meanwhile some people are simply wondering *if* they get to eat because food isn't as available for them as it should be.

Lord have merthy, it makes our heads spin.

There are lots of different opinions about food from very smart people with degrees in these sorts of things and also from randos on social media who might have no idea what they're talking about whatsoever. But two things are perfectly clear: feeding yourself doesn't have to feel stressful, and "healthy" looks different for different people.

FIVE FAST FACTS ABOUT FOOD

1. **FOOD ISN'T MORALLY BAD OR GOOD.** Food just chills in its package or produce bin, wondering why people are making all these judgment calls about it. *Let it live.* It's just a tortilla chip and hasn't done anything wrong (other than the time it got caught in Jacob's windpipe, and it already apologized about that).

2. **FOOD IS PERSONAL.** People avoid certain foods for a whole number of reasons. Some folks have to be mindful of allergies or sensitivities because particular foods affect their bodies in ways we don't want to get into. Others have simple likes and dislikes—one person's "oooh delish" activates another person's gag reflex. Still others dodge specific foods because of religion or cultural tradition. Their choices have nothing to do with yours or anyone else's. Eat what ya like!

3. FOOD IS FUEL. The cells inside our bodies are so needy. They really are. Ugh. They're in constant demand of energy, and that energy comes from food, no matter what type of food that is. A juicy medium-rare sirloin fuels your body, and so does a heaping bowl of salad, and so does the scoop of casserole the lunch workers ladle onto your tray. Without food, your cells go kaput, along with your energy, your attention span, and your ability to do life. Which means *everyone* needs to eat and deserves to have delicious food in their lives on the daily.

4. FOOD IS OFTEN PART OF CELEBRATIONS. While food keeps your cells humming, it isn't just eaten for energy. Sometimes it's a frosted birthday cake given to a one-year-old who's wondering why adults are singing loudly to them and taking pictures. Other times it's an empanada eaten during a parade to celebrate Fiestas Patrias in Chile. Or maybe it's red bean porridge consumed during the Winter Solstice in Korea. Sometimes food is a gift, a memory, or a meal to be shared with people you like to be in the same room with (for a little while at least).

5. FOOD CAN BE STRESSFUL. For many people, thinking about food ruins their whole day. Perhaps they don't know when they'll get another meal. Or maybe they have to avoid dairy. Or maybe they have a parent who never solved their food issues and now they worry about every last thing that ends up on their plate. We recognize that for some people food is simple. You get a bucket of popcorn at the movies and eat it. No big deal. But for others? Not so much.

Disordered Eating

Remember how we said food is complicated? Yeah. It is. Especially for teenagers who are facing eating disorders. And . . . you never know who that could be. Despite troll comments on social media, you cannot tell what sort of relationship someone has with food based on their gender, ethnicity, religion, identity, or the size of their body.

Did you know that eating disorders are the third-most diagnosed chronic disorder in teens? It's true! And that's just in the teens who *report* it. In the United States alone, 28.8 million Americans will deal with an eating disorder at some point in their lives. Tess is one of them.

TESS'S EATING DISORDER

Tess was diagnosed with *atypical anorexia nervosa* in 2020, though her disordered eating started around age ten.

She pinpoints one moment when she believes it began. After a family tragedy that left her mother disabled, Tess was at her aunt's house eating a bowl of Campbell's vegetable beef soup with saltine crackers. Tess put a few crackers into the soup, then a few more, and before long, she'd eaten the entire sleeve of saltines.

"It filled me up," she says. "I felt full."

She felt comforted.

In 2020 she was speaking on a panel with Anna Sweeney, our dietitian consultant for this book. Anna's message to the audience about feeding themselves based on their instincts stuck with Tess. After the conference was over, she reached out to Ms. Sweeney and asked for some help. A couple of long conversations later, Anna thought Tess might have atypical anorexia nervosa.

Tess was shocked. "Have you seen my body?" she asked her. "I'm fat!"

But Anna told her that size has nothing to do with it and referred her to a psychologist who confirmed Anna's expert opinion.

Fans and other people online 100 percent did not like hearing that Tess had an eating disorder. After pressing "send" on an infamous tweet that explained her diagnosis, trolls all over the web claimed she was a liar, which was strange because she didn't remember any of them being in the doctor's office when she was diagnosed. Anyway.

She exists in a bigger body than some people, and remember: body size is not an indicator of a person's relationship with food. There *are* some pretty good signs to look out for, though, that could give you a heads-up that something might be wrong.

WHAT IS ATYPICAL ANOREXIA NERVOSA?

It's a psychological disorder just like anxiety or depression that comes chock full with a bunch of mental and emotional distress. In fact, because the only difference between atypical anorexia and typical anorexia is body weight—those with the atypical kind have bodies that are not medically underweight—the distress related to eating and body image can be pretty darn bad, and the risks associated are the exact same. Also, atypical anorexia is much more common than anorexia. The prevalence of diagnosed atypical anorexia by age twenty is triple that of those diagnosed with anorexia.

SIGNS THAT YOU (OR A FRIEND) MIGHT NEED TO TALK TO A PROFESSIONAL ABOUT FOOD

Besides atypical anorexia, there are a bunch of other eating disorders out there that should all be diagnosed by a doctor and not by Todd from TikTok or your bestie who saw a video about it one time. Here are some of the disorders that can affect teens, according to the American Academy of Pediatrics:

• Anorexia nervosa

• Bulimia nervosa

• Binge eating disorder

• Other specified feeding and eating disorders (OSFED)

• Avoidant restrictive food intake disorder (ARFID)

Each one takes a sledgehammer to a person's feelings about eating and comes with its own symptoms and mental, emotional, and physical side effects. If you're wondering whether you or a friend might be dealing with any of them, look at the following list. These are just some of the signs that you might need to talk to a doctor:

• Feeling pretty bad about yourself in general

• Focusing constantly on body weight, size, and shape—and less on other things

• Being super scared about gaining weight or having fat on your body

• Fixating on meals, calories, protein, fat content, and so on

• Not allowing yourself to eat freely

• Compensating for something you've eaten

• Hiding what you eat

• Feeling more irritable or moody than ever

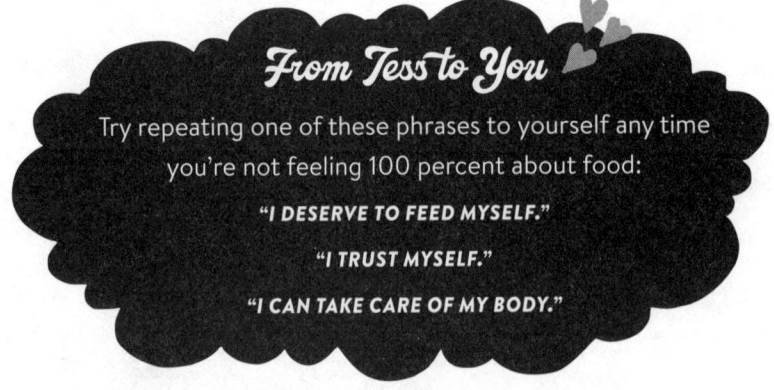

From Jess to You

Try repeating one of these phrases to yourself any time you're not feeling 100 percent about food:

"I DESERVE TO FEED MYSELF."

"I TRUST MYSELF."

"I CAN TAKE CARE OF MY BODY."

Resources That
Can Help Anyone

Whether your goal is going toe-to-toe with an eating disorder, getting some food in your mouth because you don't have enough, or simply learning how to try new cuisines, there's help! Never fear! (One caveat: new foods can be tasty as heck, as long as you aren't allergic to them. We don't wanna see any eyes swollen shut. So if you're not sure whether you're allergic to say, cantaloupe, then check with someone who knows your health history.)

I Need to Talk to Someone About a Suspected Eating Disorder

- **IF YOU NOTICE A FRIEND SHOWING SIGNS:** Ms. Sweeney suggests saying things like, "I've noticed that something has changed about how you talk about your body or the food we're eating. I'm worried about you because I care. Can we get you some help?"

- **IF YOU'RE THE ONE SHOWING SIGNS:** Ms. Sweeney says to take these steps:
  - **STEP 1:** Congratulate yourself for recognizing that things aren't quite right. That's a major step!
  - **STEP 2:** Find a trusted friend or adult to talk to. Whether that's a caregiver, school counselor, parent, favorite teacher, coach, community leader, religious leader, or a neighbor who lets you cut through their yard, tell someone.
  - **STEP 3:** Say it clearly: "Things are not okay for me. I need help related to how I feel about food."
  - **STEP 4:** Together or solo, go to the National Alliance for Eating Disorders website (www.allianceforeatingdisorders.com). You can call someone today.

I Need Better Access to Food

- **TALK TO AN ADULT WHO MAKES YOU FEEL SAFE.** Tell them you're hungry. They can help you! It takes bravery to fight for yourself. We know that. But you should never be ashamed to ask. We all need help from time to time.

- **VISIT A FOOD DONATION WEBSITE.** Do an online search for "food pantries near me." A food pantry is a place dedicated to giving food completely free to anyone who's hungry, regardless of their identity, social status, or income. Many churches, synagogues, mosques, and other houses of worship have them set up and ready to go. You can also check out sites like NoKidHungry.org and Fullcart.org. They provide food directly to your home or tell you where to get free food over school breaks and during the summer.

YOU CAN MAKE AN IMPACT

If you know kids at your school who don't get dinner and that's not okay with you, consider starting a school food pantry with the help of a teacher or another adult sponsor. Take donations and make bags with snacks and microwave dinners. Kids can grab the bags from a teacher's room on their way home.

I Want to Try New Foods

- **KEEP THE PRESSURE LOW.** If you're interested in trying something new, maybe now is not the time to hit up a restaurant you've never been to before and order a plate of food you've never seen, let alone tasted. Consider adding just one new food to your plate, and surround it with food you already like. That way, you won't be hungry if that particular bite didn't agree with you.

- **GET INSPIRED BY A CULTURE DIFFERENT FROM YOURS.** Even if you've never tried anything other than the food you grew up eating, do a little YouTubing or Pinteresting to look up some recipes to cook or places to buy foods similar to stuff you already like.

IF YOU LIKE . . .	TRY . . .	WHY?
Chicken noodle soup	Vietnamese pho	They're both noodles in broth with vegetables.
Italian calzones	Greek spanakopita, Colombian empanadas, or Indian samosas	They're all some sort of dough stuffed with tasty ingredients.
Thai or Indian curry	Ethiopian wat	All are spicy stews made with ingredients like meat and vegetables.
French baguettes	Chinese baozi, Algerian khobz el dar, Irish soda bread, German pumpernickel, or Mozambican pão	Because bread is yum and yum is bread.
Belgian chocolate truffles	Brazilian brigadeiro	They're both chocolate spheres that melt in your mouth.

A Final Word on Feeding Yourself

Eating a good meal and then snuggling up to watch Netflix with your favorite dessert is just Friday night for some people, but it can be a major struggle for others. Ms. Sweeney says to ask yourself questions like these if you're in the latter group:

• Which foods make my body feel good?

• What do I like the taste of?

• What feels comfortable to eat?

• Which foods are important to my family or culture?

• What feels easy to eat or prepare?

• Which foods feel the least stressful?

We're here to let you know that no matter what your history with food has been, we see you, we've been there, and we're betting that there are people in your life who are willing to listen if you choose to reach out.

QUIZ TIME

Which Dessert Are You?

Answer each question and
keep track of the letters you choose.

1. Pick a texture. Any texture.

A. Crispy and gooey

B. Soft and spongy

C. Smooth and creamy

D. Crunchy and chewy

2. How expensive are your clothes?

A. I like a label, but usually it's not
that important.

B. Mid.

C. I go top tier as often as possible
because life is short!

D. I'm a thrifter. Why pay more when
you don't have to?

3. Which flavors are calling your name?

A. Cinnamon and sugar

B. Dark chocolate and coffee

C. Tart lemon and herbs

D. Caramel and vanilla

**4. The two colors that best describe
me are:**

A. Lime green and candy-apple red

B. Warm, velvety brown and chestnut

C. Lavender and butter yellow

D. Gold and caramel

5. How sweet are you?

A. Sugary sweet most of the time

B. Medium sweet with a just a little edginess
popping out from time to time

C. Sometimes sweet? But usually sarcastic
and funny.

D. My sweet is usually mixed with a little
saltiness because LIFE.

6. Pick a description of yourself.

A. I'm *always* welcome at holiday get-
togethers because everyone loves me.

B. I give every party the life it deserves.
pops a balloon

C. I'm mature and complex and get the things
I want out of life.

D. I'm a bit of a joker and enjoy the simple
things in life.

7. My room aesthetic is:

A. Light and airy with lots of homemade
touches. Think patchwork quilt and
well-loved childhood toys.

B. Snuggly and comforting with warm rugs and
thick, fur blankets.

C. Upscale and refined with impeccable taste.
This is a room on Pinterest.

D. Whatever is in there. Got a bed,
so it's fine.

8. Desserts with crust?

A. Flaky pastry crust, please and thank you

B. Crust? Who needs crust?

C. A buttery, toasted crumb crust is heavenly!

D. Maybe just the corners

9. Choose a candle to light:

A. Cinnamon Dolce

B. Hot Cocoa Nights

C. Lavender Fields

D. Warm Toasted Caramel

10. I love to eat dessert:

A. In the fall surrounded by autumn leaves

B. On Valentine's Day or at a birthday party

C. At prom or another fancy occasion

D. Literally any day of the week

Answers

IF YOU CHOSE MOSTLY A'S: You're a warm slice of apple pie with a cinnamon-sugar crust. We bet you're sweet, and people see you as wholesome and friendly.

IF YOU CHOSE MOSTLY B'S: You're a triple-chocolate cupcake. We just know you're the life of any party, think deeply about things that are important to you, and have a soft spot for others.

IF YOU CHOSE MOSTLY C'S: You're a lavender lemon tart with a toasted graham-cracker crust. We think you're glamorous, refined, and just as witty as you are kind.

IF YOU CHOSE MOSTLY D'S: You're a caramel blondie. We bet you're reliable and approachable and make other people feel safe when they're around you.

Tess's Extras

Tess's Banana Pudding Popsicles Recipe

Tess's MawMaw, the name her grandmother used, made a banana pudding dessert that reminds Tess of her home in Mississippi. This is her spin on it, and *trust us*, it's *so* good. Droolworthy, in fact! If you give it a whirl, take pics or videos and tag us on social media! @tessholliday @kellycoon106 #bananapuddingpops

BANANA PUDDING POPSICLES

From the kitchen of:

Tess Holliday, inspired by her MawMaw's banana pudding recipe

PREP TIME: 20 minutes   **TOTAL TIME:** 6 hours

INGREDIENTS:

1 box Jell-O banana pudding, or make your own!

2 cups cold milk (if using Jell-O)

2 to 3 bananas

Nilla Wafers or graham crackers, crushed

Popsicle molds and sticks

Sprinkles

STEPS:

Slice the bananas, then put them in the freezer on a sheet tray for twenty minutes so they partially freeze.

Make the pudding according to the recipe on the box, or follow your own recipe. You'll need the cold milk for the Jell-O recipe. Allow it to set for the amount of time noted on the box.

Take the bananas out of the freezer. Layer the sliced bananas, the prepared pudding, and the crushed Nilla Wafers or grahams in each popsicle mold twice.

Add sprinkles to the base of each popsicle.

Put sticks in each popsicle, and cover with foil or the mold lid. Freeze until solid—about 6 to 8 hours.

Enjoy every last mouth-watering bite!

Feed Me Discussion
QUESTIONS

1. Name a country with a cuisine you've never tried. Get out your phone, and look up a dish from that country. Describe the dish and whether you'd be willing to try it.

2. Discuss a warm and fuzzy memory that you strongly associate with food.

3. What are the best cooking shows to watch?

4. If you could only eat one cuisine from around the world for the next twenty years, which would you choose and why?

5. If nearly 30 million Americans will struggle with an eating disorder at some point in their lives, how do you think social media impacts that?

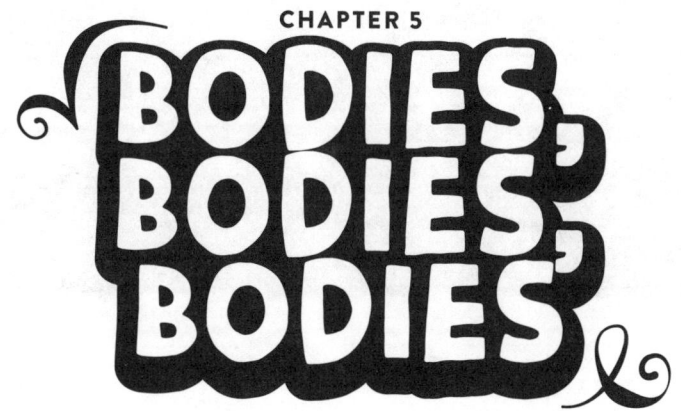

CHAPTER 5

BODIES, BODIES, BODIES

BODIES ARE A HOT TOPIC, AREN'T THEY? PEOPLE TAKE PICS of their booty cheeks or flexed biceps and post them on social media. For them, it's empowering to show off the parts of themselves they're proud of. For others who scroll past those pictures, they can be a real downer, especially if they're trying to look a certain way and aren't anywhere close in their own opinion.

Fun fact: our bodies aren't who we are. They're more like the cars that take our souls, consciousness, psyches—whatever you wanna call your inner essence—wherever we want to go, whether that's to the kitchen for a banana pudding popsicle or down the street to meet up with friends. But, if that's true, why is the roundness of our bumpers or the shape of our frames such a hot topic on social media?

One reason is dolla dolla bills, y'all.

The wellness industry—with sectors like fitness, nutrition, and weight loss—generates a whopping $5.6 trillion annually. And it's gonna bloat up to $8.5 trillion by 2027. Wellness makes money, so Studly Steve and Jacked Jazmine have cash reasons to not only take pictures of their shredded abs but also make promises that don't always pan out for the people scrolling.

RIGHT ON THE MONEY

A trillion is hard to visualize when it comes to cash, so let's do this: count to ten. Goes pretty quick, right? Well, if you counted to 1 trillion and said one number each second, it would take you 31,709.8 years to finish. Basically, your zombified corpse would be coughing out the last numbers because we haven't quite figured out how to live longer than 120 years or so. Long story short: a trillion dollars is a lot, which explains why people promoting shady wellness claims have zero incentive to stop.

The Wellness Culture

Content creators across the globe promote "health" and "healthy lifestyles" online, which sound good, but those concepts are vague, mean different things to different people, and are often completely contradictory when it comes to body size:

- Some say you should put on muscle, but others say don't get too bulky or veiny.
- Some say you should lose weight, but others say not to be too skinny.
- Some say they value "thique" physiques, but only promote certain body types.
- Some say to get your legs big and strong, but no dimples or stretch marks allowed.
- Some say you should work out daily, but others say don't be obsessed about it.

And that says nothing about the comments on the posts. Find a post of someone working hard on a treadmill, and there are dozens of trolls telling them they sweat too much or are wearing the wrong gym clothes.

And! And! Even if you decide to go hard at the gym and forget about anyone who might post videos of your efforts, you might feel like you're not quite doing it right because you should do less cardio and more weights. Or was it more HIIT and less yoga? Or no yoga and more running? So by the time you make up your mind to even go for a walk, you're terrified that you're doing it all wrong, so why even try?

Sound familiar?

Yeah. TRUST US. We get it. For some creators, it's not really about health at all. It's only about body image.

The Way You Look at Your Body

The feelings and judgments you have about your body and what you think other people believe about your body is called your *body image*. Your body image can sometimes be negative, which creates feelings of shame, distress, and general "UGHness," but it can also be positive or even neutral, where you don't really think too much about the vehicle you're driving around.

Some people on social media take advantage of negative body image, but if you know what to look for, you can weed out messaging that can damage it. Ask yourself these three questions before trusting a content creator:

1. **ARE THEY QUALIFIED TO GIVE ADVICE?** Any rando in stretch tights can post "health" content. Look for respected doctors and coaches with certifications. And even then, don't listen to them if you answer yes to questions 2 and 3.

2. **DO THEIR PROMISES SEEM TOO GOOD TO BE TRUE?** If so, they probably are. "I can change your life in ten days for $39.99" is a sales pitch, not a fact.

3. **DOES THEIR CONTENT MAKE YOU FEEL ASHAMED ABOUT YOUR BODY IN SOME WAY?** Block. Report. Tell the algo to stop showing you this stuff. A person who truly wants to help you live your very best life gives advice that is backed up by science and *never* makes you ashamed of your body.

Let's Talk About Health

According to the World Health Organization, "Health is a state of complete physical, mental, and social well-being and not merely the absence of disease or infirmity," and that means different things for different people. According to our pediatrician consultant, Dr. Nika Douvikas, physical health is made up of a *lot* of things, which *very obviously* means that we can't tell a person's health by their body shape or size.

People driving Ferraris around can be healthy, unhealthy, or somewhere in between. People driving Ford F-150s can be healthy, unhealthy, or somewhere in between. A small body is not necessarily healthy. A large body is not necessarily unhealthy.

The Genetics of Size

The wellness machine likes to say that your size is always a direct result of your habits. If you're big, you must wallow around on the couch and eat stacks of cheeseburgers at midnight. If you're thin, you must run sixteen miles a day and guzzle smoothies made of poached chicken and wheatgrass.

Harvard researchers say that's silly. While habits can impact overall health, body size isn't necessarily a reflection of the habits you have. One guy who runs every day might be bigger and have more fat cells than another guy who's never worked out in his life. Genetics are a thing. You can't always out-habit DNA that tells fat cells to sit tight because they just might be needed. Some folks in bigger bodies descended from ancestors who needed to store fat to stay alive through famines, and those genes swam on down through history and landed in their cells. In fact, this is 80 percent of the reason some people are in bigger bodies.

The myth is that bigger size equals poor health, bad habits, and a lack of effort. That can be true for some people, but researchers disagree that it's true for *all* people, and those of us on the sidelines cannot tell the difference between the two. (Side note: it's also none of our business why anyone is thin, thick, or anything in between. Just saying.)

Ten Goals for Physical Wellness

So if you can't tell how healthy you are based on the space you take up on the couch, what do pediatricians like Dr. Douvikas say to pay attention to?

This stuff:

1. Moving your body daily

2. Understanding how your body works

3. Making informed choices about your body

4. Feeling capable while moving

5. Recognizing when your body feels off in some way

6. Eating foods that make you feel good and drinking enough water

7. Sleeping enough for your age

8. Preventing illness and injury

9. Managing health conditions

10. Seeing a doctor when you need to

DOCTOR YOURSELF

Pay attention to number 5 on the list above: what your gut is telling you. If you feel like something is going on with your body—a new pain, a little spot, a funny sensation—tell someone you trust about it. You know yourself better than anyone else.

Most of us probably aren't paying attention to this list *all* the time. That's why it's a list of goals, not mandates for the perfect life or anything like that. Plus, how people approach these goals is different for everyone because people are—wait for it—*different*. Shocking, we know.

For example, Tess moves her body twenty minutes a day, while someone else might go for forty-five minutes. Some people prevent illness by scrubbing their hands often and eating a wide variety of foods, while others need to take medication to stay out of the hospital. Health decisions are as individual as people are, and none of us should judge another's health level for any reason, least of all their size.

TESS'S ADVICE FOR LIVING IN A LARGER BODY

If you *are* in a thicker body, you're not alone. Not by a long shot, even if it feels that way. Here's some of Tess's advice to help make it easier:

1. Use a smoothing stick like Body Glide or Megababe Thigh Rescue to prevent chafing between thighs or under your arms.

2. Keep all the little dips and bumps in your body clean and dry to prevent rashes. If you get a rash, get medical help before it becomes a problem.

3. Stretch . . . even if you can't do any other movement that day.

4. Big people need proper, stable footwear.

5. Live your life! You're allowed to have fun exactly as you are right now.

6. Not to be that girl, but take up space. When you're in a larger body, people can try to make you feel bad about needing a bigger seat or more room in a photo. Don't apologize for existing in the body you live in!

I Like to Move It, Move It

Moving your body is a good thing. It can be a joy, it's most certainly a privilege, and most of us can do it in big or small ways. We see you if you're not in the "most" category, where you can't move your body for whatever reason. Feeling pressured to move when you don't want to or when you simply can't because of illness, injury, health, or any other reason feels pretty dang bad. Dr. Douvikas agrees. She stresses that it's important for movement to give you a little zing of enjoyment, or else many of us will absolutely stay in bed watching reruns of *Grey's Anatomy*, instead.

The Four Most Important Types of Exercise for Those Who Are Able

TYPE	DEFINITION	BENEFITS	EXAMPLES
Strengthening	Movement that makes your muscles stronger	Improves confidence, helps you feel capable, lowers blood sugar, builds bone	Push-ups, squats, lunges, weight machines, dumbbells, bands, Pilates, etc.
Aerobic	Movement that speeds up your heart rate and breathing	Boosts your mood, gives heart and lungs a workout, increases endurance	Walking, swimming, dancing, biking, running, climbing, etc.
Stretching	Movement that helps you stay flexible	Makes muscles longer, increases range of motion, reduces the risk of injury and pain	Dynamic stretches—stretching while doing the same motion. Think arm circles, marching in place, neck rolls, etc. Static stretches—holding a position for at least sixty seconds. Think calf stretch, quad stretch, yoga stretches, etc.
Balance	Movement that helps you stay steady	Reduces the risk of injury, improves sports performance	Using a stability ball, yoga, biking, Pilates, single leg movements, etc.

Even though the word *exercise* can inspire night terrors for some people (oh nooooooo, not RUNNING! AHHHHH!), moving your body should make you feel good, not bad. There are about forty-seven thousand ways to move, and none of them have to make you panic puke. Running isn't for everyone, but there are a lot of things that might feel good to try!

MOVEMENTS THAT MIGHT NOT SUCK

1. **VR HEADSET GAMES:** Toss on a headset and laser-sword the head off a dragon. If you're moving around, it counts.

2. **DANCE:** Line dance, salsa, slam dance, or pirouette in the basement around the washing machine. If you use a wheelchair, go for a para dance class. Bonus: you get to listen to music.

3. **ROCK CLIMB:** Find an indoor rock-climbing place or a literal mountain, and have at it. Pair it with a hike, and just *breathe* in all the ways you're benefitting your body, mind, and spirit.

4. DIGITAL GEOCACHING: *Pokémon Go* will you send you four blocks west for Pidgeys, which makes your phone good for you. You heard it here first.

5. REC LEAGUE SPORTS: You don't have to be a DI athlete to play two-on-two basketball. Or wheelchair tennis. Or volleyball. Or pickleball. Or any other sport that makes you happy. You can try something new no matter how old or skilled you are.

6. BACKYARD GAMES: Invite a couple of friends over, and go absolutely feral playing capture the flag, flashlight tag, or freeze tag. Don't break an ankle in a gopher hole, though.

7. BUILD STUFF: In the winter up north, go make a snow family. If it doesn't snow where you live, build an indoor or outdoor fort for your little cousin (or yourself).

8. PLAY LASER TAG OR PAINTBALL: You don't have to be at a birthday party to battle it out. There's no *rule* about it.

9. MOVE WITH AN AUDIOBOOK OR PODCAST: Sometimes it's boring listening to music while you work out, so try a true crime podcast, a fantasy novel, or a comedy show instead.

10. USE A PULL-UP BAR: Put a pull-up bar on a doorway you go through a lot. Every time you move under it, reach up and try to do a pull-up. If you can't, just hang from it to improve your grip strength.

YOU WANT TO TRY MOVING YOUR BODY, BUT . . .

. . . YOU FEEL LIKE THE MOST UNMOTIVATED PERSON ALIVE. Movement should make you feel good from the inside out, and it's extremely important to listen to yourself. Before you toss on your gym shorts, ask yourself if you feel energetic, stiff, in need of a stretch, bored, or restless. If you answer yes to any of those, you might need to move! But sometimes rest really is what your body needs. If you find yourself longing for a nap, feeling sore, or completely disinterested, trust yourself and take a break.

. . . YOU HAVEN'T FOUND SOMETHING THAT FITS YOU VERY WELL. Your brother tells you you're bad at sports. You don't know how to use your mom's weight set in the garage and will absolutely never ask because, well, mom issues. Cool. You haven't found the right fit yet. But you won't if you don't try stuff either. You might be a yoga guru or kickboxing genius in the making. You never know until you give something a whirl!

. . . YOU'RE OVERTHINKING IT. Movement is movement, period. You don't have to put in two hours of heart-pounding power lifting at a gym filled with Studly Steves. You can literally go outside and dig a hole if you want to.

. . . YOU'RE SCARED. What if you try a machine at the gym and use it wrong? What if your muscles are smaller than other people's and you can only use baby weights? ACK. Remove half of the mental barrier by going with a friend or working out solo in your room. (YouTube exists for a reason!) Tell yourself you don't have to be perfect either. No one is born knowing how to bench press. Even Jacked Jazmine had to learn once upon a time.

. . . YOU'RE IN PAIN WHEN YOU MOVE. Immediately talk to a trusted adult who can get you in touch with a doctor. Movement shouldn't be painful, and if it is, then something might be going on that you need to deal with. STAT.

From Tess to You

I love doing Pilates because it strengthens my body and stretches me out, and it's something that makes me feel good. It was the first form of movement I didn't dread. I also like swimming, which is part of the reason I moved to the beach! You don't have to be a certain size to move.

A Final Word on Your Body

We didn't get into like 95 percent of things about this vehicle we drive around on planet Earth because there is just so much to talk about, but we do want to leave you with a couple of thoughts. Social media will you tell you that the "ideal" body is a certain size and shape. But here's the truth:

AN IDEAL BODY IS TREATED WELL.

AN IDEAL BODY IS RESPECTED.

AN IDEAL BODY GETS ENOUGH REST.

AN IDEAL BODY IS FED AND HYDRATED.

AN IDEAL BODY MOVES.

AN IDEAL BODY KNOWS WHEN TO SEEK HELP.

The body you're living in is okay just as it is. You're allowed to drive it around and chase your dreams with the current make and model. In fact, we *want* you to go after those dreams *right now*, not when you've streamlined the frame or gotten a bigger bumper.

The people who love you feel the same way too, even if they haven't said so.

QUIZ TIME

How Do You Wanna Move It?

You know the drill! Answer.
Keep track of the letters associated with your answers.

1. The best color is:

A. Black

B. Blue

C. Violet

D. Red

E. Green

2. Which type of dog is the goodest baby?

A. German shepherd

B. Border collie

C. Greyhound

D. Labrador retriever

E. Bulldog

3. On Sunday you want to:

A. Go to a park

B. Solo road trip!

C. Stretch out while browsing your phone

D. Watch some sports

E. Rearrange your bedroom

4. Your music playlist has a lot of:

A. Classical

B. Electronic

C. Indie or folk

D. Country rock

E. Hip hop

5. Where are you traveling after high school?

A. Kyoto, Japan

B. Broome, Australia

C. Montevideo, Uruguay

D. Cape Town, South Africa

E. Reykjavik, Iceland

6. What's your ride?

A. I prefer to walk.

B. Motorcycle

C. Tandem bike

D. Carpooling with friends

E. Monster truck

7. The best way to connect with people is:

A. Chilling with them quietly

B. Text messages

C. Face-to-face conversations

D. Group chats

E. Leaving voicemails

8. You like your weather:

A. Crisp and clear

B. Overcast but hot

C. Breezy and warm

D. Sunny and mild

E. Snowy and cold

9. Select a historical era to visit:

A. The Ming dynasty

B. Ancient Greece

C. The Renaissance

D. The Industrial Revolution

E. The Viking Age

10. What's for dinner?

A. Sushi rolls and clear soup

B. Lemon basil pasta with Parmesan cheese

C. Empanadas with beans and rice

D. Hamburgers and mac 'n' cheese

E. A turkey leg with a loaded baked potato

Answers

IF YOU CHOSE MOSTLY CHOSE A'S: Your exercise vibe is martial arts—precision and disciplined power fit you to a T.

IF YOU CHOSE MOSTLY CHOSE B'S: Swimming is your go-to for an individual challenge that meets your need for strength and speed.

IF YOU CHOSE MOSTLY CHOSE C'S: Partner dance is your style—grace, flexibility, and rhythm while coordinating with someone else.

IF YOU CHOSE MOSTLY CHOSE D'S: Team sports suit you—let's goooooo, extroverts who like group challenges and competition!

IF YOU CHOSE MOSTLY CHOSE E'S: Weight lifting is your thing—strength and stamina for the win.

It's the Write Time

Time to spill! Pull up your Notes app on your phone or open up a paper journal, and answer these questions:

1. If you could instantly be an expert in some physical activity—think anything from ice hockey to rock climbing to aerial acrobatics to MMA Fighting—what would it be?

2. How does this connect with who you are as a person?

3. Which of your personal strengths could help you really get into that activity?

Bodies, Bodies, Bodies Discussion
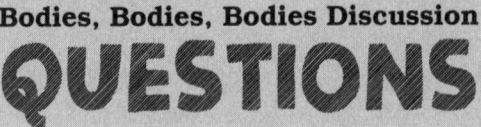

1. Discuss whether the government should regulate social media because of the negative impact it can have on body image.

2. Some places—like some airplanes, stadium seating, and theaters—don't have seating that accommodates larger bodies. How important is it to make sure everyone has a seat they're comfortable in?

3. Which of these activities sounds like the most fun to try? Flying the trapeze in a circus, rock climbing Mount Rainier, horseback riding on a beach, or paddle boarding in the Caribbean Ocean?

4. Which social media content creator or celebrity seems to have a positive influence on people's beliefs about themselves? How do they accomplish this?

5. If you had to rate your own body image—or how you feel about your body—on a scale of 1 to 5, with 1 being poor and 5 being excellent, what number would you choose and why?

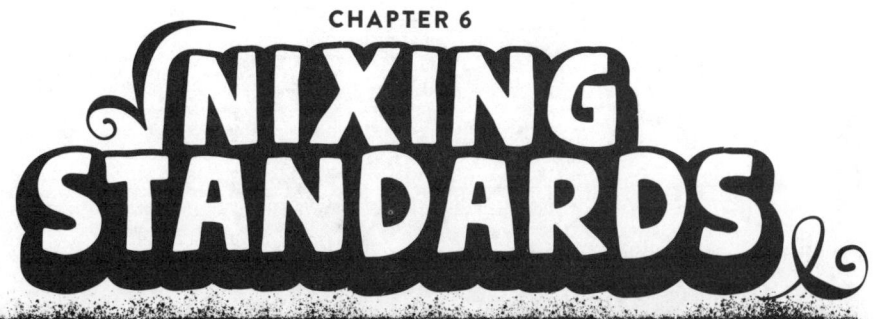

CHAPTER 6

NIXING STANDARDS

KELLY: Hey, Tess, wanna talk about the reason you started a movement against the beauty industry?

TESS: Of course. Literally what I breathe for.

KELLY: Yesss. So tell me: How did the whole "Eff Your Beauty Standards" hashtag on Instagram come to be?

TESS: Well, I was on Tumblr one day posting stuff, and per usual, people were coming out from underneath their rocks to say mean things about me. They were telling me what I should and shouldn't wear in public. Saying I should cover up my arms. Telling me not to wear a bathing suit, blah blah blah.

KELLY: Gross.

TESS: Right? So that day I was just sick of it. I went to bed because I was over it. I felt like, *You know what? Eff this. I'm tired of everyone telling me what I can and can't wear and what I should and shouldn't do.* I couldn't post one photo without people trying to make me feel bad for existing. So . . . I went on Instagram.

KELLY: As one does.

TESS: Haha, yes. I posted something like, "If you're tired of everyone dictating how you should look, what you should wear, etc., post a picture of yourself wearing something that makes you feel good or scares you, and use the hashtag #effyourbeautystandards." I posted a picture, and before I knew it, it took off. People of all sizes started posting photos and videos of themselves, and it never stopped. It became an entire movement online, and I started the Instagram handle with the same name to make sure people had a safe place to go. Now it's been shared more than 4 million times on Instagram alone.

KELLY: That's a ton! So it changed how people presented themselves online?

TESS: It did. It empowered people. They felt like they could put on something they wouldn't normally wear because other people were doing it too. It gave them the power to feel good about how they wanted to show up in the world. I mean, it's just silly to tell other people what they're allowed to wear, and this showed it.

KELLY: That's amazing, Tess.

TESS: It really is. I'm shocked. I never expected it to go viral.

KELLY: How did you feel about it once it did?

TESS: Less alone. I needed community and solidarity. Living in a body that's outside of average can be really, really hard. And it made me and millions of other people feel better to know that we weren't the only ones feeling that way or—I don't know—exasperated by the current beauty climate. It fueled me to be less afraid about just existing in the space I live in.

The Wildflowers of Humanity

It's bizarre that there are even beauty standards at all, because people are super different from each other. Think about it. There are 195 nations on Earth. Each one is stuffed full of people with different abilities, skin colors, body sizes, ethnicities, hair types, and facial features. If you take skin tone alone, and mix just that one feature with another, like body size, you're looking at kabillions of different ways a person could look. Think about how boring it would be if you went into a flower shop and all they carried were daisies.

What's beautiful to one country, one culture, or even one person could be the complete opposite of what's beautiful to another. So it makes no sense when companies shove "beauty" into a teeny-tiny box, because not everyone is gonna fit in there.

Take the modeling business, for instance. You'd think that companies would want to use models that represent real-life people to show how clothes or makeup or whatever might look on them, but wildly enough, that isn't true (most of the time). Let's look at some numbers, shall we?

GROUPS OF PEOPLE	PERCENTAGE OF U.S. POPULATION	PERCENTAGE OF FASHION MODELS
Males	49.6%	22.3%
Women wearing a size 14 or above	67%	2%[1] in all media 1% walked in 2023 NY fashion week
People with disabilities	24%	0.02%
Women who are 5'9" or taller	3.4%	95%+
People with eating disorders	9%	40%

[1] Isabel Angell and Ethan Oberman, "Closing the Representation Gap for Plus-Size Women," *The Takeaway*, September 28, 2016, Accessed December 4, 2023. https://www.wnycstudios.org/podcasts/takeaway/segments/closing-representation-gap-plus-size-women.

Most models aren't an accurate representation of the average human, and newsflash: neither are some social media influencers who use excessive filters or Photoshop to put themselves in the exact same advertising boxes. This is a darn shame, because it sets people up to believe that in order to be beautiful, you must look a certain way. That idea is false as heck, because beauty standards change depending on lots of things, starting with your actual birth year.

Beauty Standards Across History

Cute crop tops and jogger pants in the twenty-first century would probably cause a pilgrim in the seventeenth century to stroke out. Beauty and body standards have *changed* over the years, people. In major ways. Check this out:

DECADE	MAKEUP AND FACIAL HAIR	HAIR	CLOTHES
1960s	• opaque eye shadow • winged eyeliner • pale lipstick • clean shaved or long goatees • soul patches	• bouffants • pixie cuts • long natural hair • pompadours • slicked back with a ducktail • The Beatles shag	• miniskirts • fringe and leopard print • berets and white boots • babydoll dresses • flared pants • vibrant block print • mod and space-age looks
1970s	• glowing skin • natural blush and eyebrows • glitter for evenings • horseshoe mustaches or bushy beards	• afros • long hair, parted in the middle • feathered hair • the shag	• bell bottoms • platform shoes • high waists • spiky collars • tie-dye anything • bright patterns and flowery prints

DECADE	MAKEUP AND FACIAL HAIR	HAIR	CLOTHES
1980s	• bright eyeshadows • neon lipsticks • thick eyeliner • faux moles • thick Tom Selleck mustaches or clean shaved	• the mullet • big hair: bangs and spiral curls • hairspray • side ponytails • braids with beads	• spandex • cut-off shirts • punk accessories • shoulder pads • high-waisted pants • ruffles • tight denim • shirts worn open to the mid-chest
1990s	• thin arched eyebrows • brown, lined matte lips • matte skin • shimmery eyeshadow • goatees • soul patches	• frosted tips • long on top with undercuts • side parts • choppy layers (The Rachel) • messy finger waves • micro braids • Fulani braids	• slip dresses • plaid flannel shirts • overalls • board shorts • baggy jeans • cropped tops
2000s	• heavy colored eyeliner • glossy lips • pale, sparkly eyeshadow • white inner corners of eyes • 5 o'clock shadow plus a little more	• chunky highlights • flat-ironed straight hair • feathered braids • spiky hair • faux hawks • flipped out ends • side parts • butterfly clips	• cargo pants • ballet flats • low-rise pants • velour pantsuits • trucker hats • camouflage • vests • chains • culottes
2010s	• smoky eyes • block brows • highlighter • contouring • long, thick beards	• defined curls • man buns • undercuts • ombre dye • box braids • beachy waves • middle parts • extensions	• athleisure • fitted tees • infinity scarves • mid-calf boots • chunky dad sneakers and wedge sneakers • skinny jeans • statement necklaces
2020s	• lashes • fresh glowy skin • bold, laminated, or brushed-up brows • overlined lips with glossy finish • contouring • any length of groomed beard	• natural brushed waves • skin fade • TikTok shag • the wolf cut • soft highlights • return of The Rachel • jeweled hair accessories • super-defined curls	• oversized sweatsuits in neutrals • cottagecore • preppy looks • maximalism • micro shorts • coquette • babydoll dresses • baggy denim • sneakers with everything

DID YOU KNOW?

Different countries have had their own sets of beauty rules throughout history. During the Heian period in Japan, some people blackened their teeth with a tincture. In the late 1700s in France, people powdered their skin white then painted blue lines on top to look veiny. From ancient history to today in the Bodi tribe in southern Ethiopia, the man with the biggest belly is the most attractive.

Body Types Are Trending: Eww

It's not just makeup and hair and clothes that go in and out of style because people can't make up their minds. Nope. You're not gonna believe this, but body types can actually be in or out of style because people *love* to be weird. Here are the women's bodies that were thought of as "ideal" in each decade for the past sixty years:

1960s: petite and delicate

1970s: long and willowy

1980s: tall and athletic

1990s: ultra-thin with round backsides

2000s: thin but toned

2010s: curvy up top, narrow waists with big backsides

2020s: trim and muscular

Men's bodies aren't thought of in quite the same way as women's, but for men it was considered "ideal" throughout history to be plump to show that you had cash money to buy food. In the 1960s and 1970s in the United States, however, it became popular to be very thin, with or without muscles. It wasn't until the 1980s that big, powerful muscles came into fashion and then went right back out in the 1990s in favor of a more average-looking build. Today gym bros have decided that men need to have eight-pack abs, though lots of other people prefer dad bods or average builds.

From Tess to You

I don't believe in rules. We make our own rules for our own bodies. Body-type trends do a lot of damage and hurt entire generations and communities, so treat your body well and ignore the rest.

Why Beauty Standards Are Goofy

If you're muscular like the 2020s tell you to be, you would not be considered "ideal" if you teleported to the 1960s. If you're into baggy sweatpants and sweatshirts, but suddenly they go out of style tomorrow because a social media influencer tells you that baggy stuff is *over*, ya loser, you might as well just call in sick to life and hang out in your room for the foreseeable future because you can't win no matter what you do.

Beauty is relative, friends, and your body doesn't have to be aesthetic anyway. Trying to meet a standard of beauty that changes based on where and when you live is like putting on a blindfold, throwing a dart, and assuming you'll hit the bull's-eye. Good luck to you and everyone else's eyeballs near the target.

WHAT MAKES SOMEONE TRULY BEAUTIFUL?

We all know there are faces that get smiled at by babies more than others. That there are people who are just cute, though we might not be able to say why exactly. But we *also* know people with looks delivered by pixie dust and starlight who we wouldn't want to be alone with for three seconds because their insides don't match their outsides.

BEAUTIFUL PEOPLE . . .

. . . show kindness.

. . . help others.

. . . believe in themselves.

. . . are patient.

. . . are happy when other people succeed.

. . . keep trying.

Yeah, we know that's kind of the same thing as your grandma telling you you're so handsome in your new shirt even when you feel like dog vomit. We've all been there. But it's true. Beauty from within will always, always, always impact what others think about you, and it will a thousand percent impact what you think about yourself, which is the most important thing.

A Final Word on Nixing Standards

After you get yourself ready for the day, you might think you didn't do enough to make yourself look good enough. Surely someone is going to see you and think, *blehhh, no thanks.*

Not only are you good enough exactly how you are, but most people aren't even thinking about you at all because they're worried about what other people think about them! It's true! You might believe that other kids have it out for you, but the truth is that half of all teens have self-confidence issues. That means they're not really thinking about whether your outfit's gonna get you dragged, because they're wondering if *their* outfit's gonna get *them* dragged.

You get to decide what beauty means for you. Never let anyone make you believe that your beauty isn't the right kind, because the world needs *every* type of flower in it, not just the daisies.

QUIZ TIME

What Beauty Vibe Are You Giving?

You know what to do!

1. Pick an outfit:

A. Tailored top with high-waisted pants

B. Flowy dress with a wide-brimmed hat

C. Leather jacket with distressed denim

D. Oversized sweatshirt and shorts

E. Crop top or tee with baggy jeans
   or sweatpants

2. Which hairstyle are you going with?

A. A sleek look

B. Loose curls

C. Vibrant streaks

D. Braids

E. A shag

3. Your nails are:

A. Nude with a subtle French tip

B. Earth toned

C. Matte black

D. Exactly like they've been since birth

E. Stiletto shaped with bold, bright colors

4. You take care of your face with:

A. A three-step skincare routine

B. DIY honey and avocado face mask

C. Chemical peels and experimental
   treatments

D. Gentle cleanser and moisturizer

E. Monthly facials and luxury
   skincare products

**5. If you had to choose a way to move
   your body, you would:**

A. Practice yoga

B. Trail run in nature

C. Do some high-intensity interval training
   (HIIT) classes

D. Take a stroll around the neighborhood

E. Weightlift at the gym with friends

6. If you listen to rap, you go with:

A. Nicki Minaj or Kendrick Lamar

B. Chance the Rapper or Anderson .Paak

C. Linkin Park or Run-D.M.C.

D. Megan Thee Stallion or Drake

E. Cardi B or Travis Scott

**7. If you had to choose one of these for
   lunch, you'd go with:**

A. Quinoa, roasted veggies, and grilled salmon

B. Vegan sushi rolls with miso soup

C. Thai red curry with extra heat

D. Homemade chicken noodle soup

E. A bacon burger with onion rings

8. On your lips it's:

A. Red or nude matte lipstick daily

B. Lip balm for a natural look

C. Metallic or unconventional lip colors

D. Nothing!

E. Dark or bold lip shades for a statement look

9. **You grabbed these shoes out of your closet:**

A. Whatever looks best with your outfit

B. Crocs or Birks

C. Combat boots

D. Ballet flats or loafers

E. The best sneakers on the planet

10. **When you want to take care of yourself, you:**

A. Read or debate with friends about all kinds of topics

B. Take a walk or chill at home

C. Do something adventurous or play video games

D. Cozy up with your favorite movie or get everyone together for a game night

E. Treat yourself to a dinner out and a shopping trip

Answers

IF YOU CHOSE MOSTLY A'S, YOUR VIBE IS INTELLIGENCE. You're giving classic. Sophisticated. Thoughtful. Your beauty comes from knowing how to make choices that reflect that brilliant mind.

IF YOU CHOSE MOSTLY B'S, YOUR VIBE IS COMPASSION. You're giving bohemian. Free spirited. Your beauty comes from putting natural and sustainable choices first, which just radiates all the love you have for the world.

IF YOU CHOSE MOSTLY C'S, YOUR VIBE IS RESILIENCE. You're giving edgy. Fearless. Your beauty comes from effortlessly embracing adventure and showcasing your amazing ability to bounce back.

IF YOU CHOSE MOSTLY D'S, YOUR VIBE IS KINDNESS. You're giving comfy. Down to earth. Your beauty comes from making other people feel safe and welcome, no matter who they are.

IF YOU CHOSE MOSTLY E'S, YOUR VIBE IS CONFIDENCE. You're giving trendy. Bold. Your beauty reflects your confident and poised personality, which causes everyone to look to you for leadership.

Draw It Out

Time to doodle! Get out some markers or crayons and a pencil. Get a sheet of paper, and fold it in half width-wise.

On the top half, draw the part of your outer self that you're secretly happy about. Maybe it's the shape of your hands or the way your eyes crinkle at the corners when you smile. It doesn't have to be perfect!

On the bottom half, draw a picture of an object that represents how you feel when someone gives you a compliment. Maybe a shooting star, a pair of mirror sunglasses, a disco ball, or a springtime thunderstorm.

Nixing Standards Discussion
QUESTIONS

1. What does beauty mean to people in your family and culture?

2. What is the thing you love about yourself the most?

3. If you had to wear the fashion trends from a particular decade, which decade would you choose, and what would you wear?

4. Beauty is relative, so what makes someone outwardly beautiful to you? What makes someone inwardly beautiful?

5. Discuss whether you feel pressure to fit in with the fashion or beauty norms at your school, at work, at home, or in another context.

All About Tess's Tattoos

KELLY: Before we jump into Part 2, can we just pause and talk about your tattoos? It's one of the first things I noticed about you, outside of that gorgeous hair, of course. First, how many do you even have? I tried to count and couldn't.

TESS: I have no idea. I mean, what counts as a tattoo? Do you count the sleeve on my arm as one or all of them individually? If we counted each little design, there would be hundreds.

KELLY: Which was the first?

TESS: A faerie on my shoulder in watercolor pink, purple, green, and blue. It was done by an ex-con named Mick who worked in a tiny shop in Mississippi.

KELLY: Haha, of course it was. But why a faerie?

TESS: I was going through a faerie phase, and of course there was fae slander after I got my tattoo. I'm glad that faerie gardens came back in so they can get the justice they deserve.

KELLY: I think all of us went through a fae phase back in the day.

TESS: It's kind of a rite of passage.

KELLY: It is. So that was the first, but which tattoo makes you laugh the most?

TESS: The ones my kiddo Bowie drew for me. He drew a crazy cactus and another one called Tomato Man, which is a tomato with legs, a face, and arms.

KELLY: Awwww.

TESS: They're both so cute. The tattoo artist actually displayed Tomato Man on the wall with the very best tattoos from the shop.

KELLY: Okay, I love that? It must make you proud every time you see it.

TESS: It really does.

KELLY: What's another one you're proud of?

TESS: My Miss Piggy tattoo, because when you're in a larger body and tattoo a figure that people have joked about because of her size, it was like taking my power back, you know? When they see her, people laugh and smile in a positive way. And it's nice to get that reaction when I'm used to people treating me the opposite.

KELLY: That's pretty powerful. Are there any others that have deeper meaning for you?

TESS: Yes. The ones I had designed for my grandparents on the backs of my legs. For my MawMaw, I have a hummingbird with a box of chocolates and a diamond. For my PawPaw, I have cowboy boots, a cowboy hat, a rope, and an oil rig.

KELLY: Did they hurt? It sounds like a lot of ink at one time.

TESS: Not as much as the ones on my shins. I almost got sick! Or the top of my foot. That hurt like crazy too.

KELLY: I bet. I don't have a single tattoo, unless you count my micro-bladed eyebrows. Haha!

TESS: You should get one!

KELLY: I always said I'd get one after my first novel came out—maybe a little moth to signify the cover of *Gravemaidens*—but I think I'm a big baby.

TESS: Don't be scared. They're really not horrible, and they can mean a lot, like the charm bracelet tattoo I got for my mom. When I was little she bought me one, so when I see it, it reminds me of her and that memory.

KELLY: I'm always worried about regret, though. Do you look back and go, "Ughhh, I'm so mad I got whatever tattoo"?

TESS: I don't love the inside of one of my arms. The guy did it too heavy, so it's blurry. But to be fair, it's a cover-up times seven, so it was going to be little bit of a mess. With that being said, every tattoo is a part of me. I try not to regret anything because I have good stories about all of them.

KELLY: Good point, good point. Maybe I'm convinced!

TESS: If you wanna go, I'll take you.

KELLY: Haha, perfect! Maybe when you get another one.

TESS: Listen, I love my tattoos, so there will absolutely be more coming!

PART 2

LOVE YOUR INNER YOU

"SEE YOUR-
SELF IN FUTURE
TENSE. YOU
MIGHT NOT
LOVE WHO YOU
ARE IN THE
PRESENT, BUT
THE FUTURE
YOU IS THRIV-
ING. TAKE ONE
STEP TO BE
THAT PERSON
TODAY."

—TESS HOLLIDAY

CHAPTER 7

CALL ME THIS, NOT THAT

WHEN KAI WAS A BABY, HE HAD THE SWEETEST LITTLE ROLLS and chubby cheeks. Out of affection, his parents nicknamed him Big Chonk. At nine, bigger and taller than all his classmates, his parents signed him up for tackle football. When they chanted his nickname from the sidelines, a couple of his teammates took notice and chanted it too, but when *they* did it, cruelty lit up their eyes. That's when it first began to dawn on Kai that he was different from the other boys in a way they thought was bad.

He began to hate the nickname.

As he got older he did his best to shrug off the taunts so he could focus on being the best football player he could be. On his seventh-grade team, he got positioned at center, even though he wanted to play tight end more than anything. He practiced his footwork at home and ran plays with his dad in the backyard, but his coaches just slapped him on the back and said his size made him O-line forever.

When he was a freshman in high school, the quarterback, Marcel, was ruthless to him. He teased him constantly about his nickname, patted his belly, and did the "Chonk" dance, which involved waddling like a penguin. Kai told him to stop, repeatedly—even "accidentally" knocked him into the lockers one day to put some muscle behind his words.

But Marcel wouldn't let up.

During a semi-finals game Kai decided he'd had enough. He refused to guard Marcel after snapping the ball, let the defense blow right past him, and got Marcel sacked three times. After their defeat, Marcel was pissed. He shouldered past Kai—hard—as they walked off the field. Kai, bursting with bitterness, took him to the ground. The fight left Marcel with a busted lip and a black eye; it left Kai with a football suspension and a trip to a counselor for anger issues.

Counseling helped Kai tell his parents how he felt. Playing center when he didn't want to. Being made fun of for his size. Even the nickname they'd given him. They were shocked! They'd given his nickname out of affection, not unkindness. But the counselor explained that the label they gave him shaped the environment in which he grew up, affecting Kai's life in a major way.

Let's Chat Labels

Listen. Kai didn't get a choice about the label his parents gave him as a baby. None of us do. If we start out as Sweetum with the Big Bum, we might be called Sweetum forever, unless we ask our parents to knock it off (and you definitely can do that—we'll show you how in a few).

For now, let's talk about the labels you give yourself. You probably already have some you use. Labels can be related to interests, jobs, personality, birth month, religion, culture, identity, nationality, sexual orientation, age, social class, body size, race, gender—you name it. Labels can be a shortcut to who you are, which is nice because it would probably be hard to constantly explain the ins and outs of your enthusiasm for badminton. Also, when you pick a label, you get to influence the way people think about you, which can be both good *and* bad.

There are literally thousands of labels you can wear, but here are a few examples so you know what we're getting at:

ABILITY AT SCHOOL LABELS
Advanced • ESL student • Honor student •
Not a good test taker • Smart • Talktative

BIRTHDAY OR AGE LABELS
Dragon baby • Gemini • Gen Z • Leo • Old soul • Teen

CULTURAL, RACIAL, OR LOCALE LABELS
Black • From the Northeast • Latina • Polynesian American • Texan • White

GENDER OR SEXUAL ORIENTATION LABELS

Female • Hetero • He/him • Nonbinary • Queer • Straight

INTEREST OR JOB LABELS

Gamer • Hot Topic sales clerk • In the band • Future doctor • Reader • Swiftie

DESCRIPTION LABELS

A good friend • Confident • Guy's guy • Helpful • Introvert • Rebel

PHYSICAL LABELS

Curly girl • Disabled • Fat • Nearsighted • Short king • Wheelchair user

RELIGIOUS LABELS

Atheist • Catholic • Christian • Hindi • Jewish • Muslim

SOCIAL CLASS LABELS

Blue collar • Lower class • Middle class •
Rich rich • Upper class • White collar

THREE GIGANTIC IMPACTS OF LABELS

1. Labels Can Change How People See Us

Maybe Kai introduces himself to someone like this: *"Hey! I'm Kai. I'm a Christian and a white guy from Texas. I'm an introvert from a working-class family, a gamer, and a football center."*

Automatically people will assume things about Kai based on the labels he uses. They might make *different* assumptions if Kai used different labels: *"Hey, I'm Kai. I'm a nonbinary sixteen-year-old from California. I'm a Taekwondo black belt, a Swiftie, and an honor student with an old soul."*

Did you picture two different people in your head when you read both descriptions? Did you make any assumptions about either one based on their labels? If so, that's pretty normal. Our brains form instant pictures to help us make quick decisions, which is helpful when a life is on the line. For instance, if we see a knife sitting on the edge of a table, we think *danger*, so we put it back in the knife block. But while it's kinda natural to form pictures about people based on labels, it can cause us to make lightning-fast assumptions, which can be inaccurate, harmful, or hurtful.

Let's see what you picture in your head with these labels:

- A teacher
- A police officer
- A powerlifter
- A doctor
- A cheerleader
- A criminal

Think about the way you connected those labels with an image without even thinking about it. Who did you picture as a teacher? What about a doctor? What gender were each of those? How about a cheerleader? Did you make any assumptions about their ability, age, race, or body size? Now what about the criminal? What image popped into your head?

CHALLENGE YOUR BRAIN

Choose a different gender for the doctor. A different race for the cheerleader. A different age for the criminal. A different body size for the police officer. A different physical ability for the teacher. We become better thinkers when we challenge the first knee-jerk assumption we make about anyone.

2. Labels Can Be Positive

Not to get all magical on you, but the language we use can literally change our reality. It can, believe it or not, make us act buck wild in class or cause us to help out with dinner, which is why choosing how you talk about yourself or even think about yourself is super important.

Positive labels are those that make you feel powerful or cozy inside, like a pile of warm puppies. Thinking of yourself as generous, kind, capable, or strong actually causes you to be more generous, kind, capable, and strong. It's true! What you believe can influence what you become.

Let's test this with an experiment, shall we? Give yourself these three labels today:

- I'm kind.
- I'm capable.
- I'm courageous.

Keep these three phrases in your back pocket and repeat them to yourself. Then tomorrow morning decide whether they actually helped you *feel* that way. If they didn't, keep trying and give it a few weeks. See if it changes the way you see yourself.

From Tess to You

Try labeling other things positively too. "I'm having a great day" or "This party's going to be fun" or "I'm not nervous. I'm excited." These shifts can flip a switch in your brain and make you feel better about whatever is going on. Get delusional. It really does help!

3. Labels Can Be Negative

Obviously, it works the opposite way too. If you're always giving yourself a hard time—saying or thinking things like, *I'm a loser, I'm stupid, I'm worthless, I'm weak,* and so on—you're going to start believing that. Just like you associate a certain person with "teacher" or "police officer," you'll start associating yourself with that negative label. The brain is a big bully like that. It likes to push us around. But we push back harder! Grrr.

Before you start calling yourself negative names, ask yourself these questions:

• **IS THIS A FACT, OR WOULD SOMEONE ELSE HAVE A DIFFERENT OPINION?** If you're not sure, ask your friends and family. Literally. Say, "Am I worthless? Because I feel that way. A lot." Chances are good they won't agree with you and might show you where your thinking has gone off the rails.

• **IS THIS WHO I ACTUALLY AM, OR DID I JUST MAKE A MISTAKE?** You're not a loser if you failed a test. It isn't who you *are.* You're human, and humans fail from time to time. Calling yourself a negative name after failure means you're more likely to make the same mistake again in the future. It's dropping a twenty-pound weight on your toe then picking it back up and dropping it again. Double whammy.

• **WHAT HAVE I DONE IN THE PAST THAT PROVES ME WRONG?** Do you call yourself stupid? Think through it. Were you stupid when you solved a problem for a friend when they were stuck? Were you stupid when you easily thought through a situation and made a great decision? Logic can be your friend here.

• **WHO WOULD I BE WITHOUT THAT LABEL?** Imagine you can't shake free from whatever negative label you've given yourself. Try thinking of who you *could* be if you didn't have it attached to you. How would you feel? What might you be able to do? Would that make you feel better or worse than how you feel right now?

Tess's Use of the Label "Fat"

KELLY: You've said in the past that you've embraced the word "fat" as a label for yourself. Now, that's a choice, because people use it in a negative way all the time.

TESS: Yeah, at first I did it to just be honest. I'm actually living in a body that's fat. That's an observation. And then if someone called me fat in a negative way, like they do on a daily basis, it wasn't a shock. Like duh. Everyone knows. Wow, you have eyes? Cool.

KELLY: Makes sense! It's sort of like some people in the LGBTQIA+ community labeling themselves as "queer." It used to be a slur, but now some people are proud to use it.

TESS: Exactly. So I used "fat" and was proud to use it, but now, I'm not sure how I feel. I've probably internalized some of the hate that goes along with that word, to be honest. So, while it has been empowering because it's shut down about a zillion trolls on my social media, it also means that I have to work extra hard to combat those negative thoughts about myself.

KELLY: Our brains are WIYALD. Constantly trying to trip us up, and for *what*?

TESS: Constantly!

KELLY: Even as adults, we have to work on this stuff. I battle that negative labeling too. My go-to is: *Wow, what a failure.* I have to use logic to fight that one all the time. It can be tough to get over. I wish sometimes that I'd started sooner. Why didn't anyone tell us this as teens, Tess? Why? We would have had longer to practice and would be experts at this point.

TESS: Wait, we *are* experts. Let's call ourselves that. Our brains will start believing it, right?

KELLY: YES! Haha! Very good point.

Someone Labeled Me the Wrong Way

Okay, but what about people like Kai? It's all well and good to choose your own labels, but Kai's parents nicknamed him "Big Chonk." What do you do if someone *else* labels you as something like a troublemaker. A loser. A failure. Fat. Ugly. Desperate. How do you change the labels someone else gives you?

Calling In

One way to handle it is to use the "calling in" technique. It's similar to calling out someone, but that's done in front of other people right when bad stuff is going down. A kid from your class calls you "fat" at lunch, which makes you mad. You pull out your phone, start recording, and tell them to knock it off loudly. You tell everyone what they did and demand an apology. Calling them out in that moment or interrupting their bad behavior and stopping further harm to yourself *can* be effective.

Orrrrrrr (and we don't have to tell you this) it can make the situation worse. *Much* worse.

Sometimes people double down when they're publicly dragged. When you call them out, they go even lower to save face. Not only do they keep calling you fat, but now they toss breadsticks at you. They stuff half-eaten food in your locker. They get an entire group of people to oink at you in the hallway. And pretty soon you're mad at yourself for saying anything at all.

What else can you do when someone labels you and you don't like it? Hide during lunch? Ignore it and pretend you're not miserable? Get your friend Kai to throw them in the trash? If your goal is to get someone to stop, maybe don't choose violence, and try this instead:

SEVEN CALL-IN STEPS

1. **ASK TO SPEAK TO THEM LATER.** Talking with them once your emotions have simmered down will make it easier for you to talk and, hopefully, for them to listen.

2. **GO ONE-ON-ONE.** They might listen better if they don't have to show off for other people.

3. **THANK THEM FOR AGREEING TO TALK TO YOU, AND TELL THEM THEY'RE "NICE" FOR DOING SO.** Giving them a positive label like "nice" helps them see themselves that way, which can nudge them in the direction of being a better listener.

4. GET CURIOUS. Ask them *why* they used that label on you and whether they were trying to be hurtful. They might have been attempting to joke around and it came off badly. Or they were just parroting what kids or even parents have said to them. It might help you realize that they're not just a nasty human who loves being a jerk.

5. TELL THEM HOW THE LABEL MAKES YOU FEEL. Use "I" language when you do it so you don't put them on the defensive. Say, "I feel upset when you call me _____," instead of "You're cruel when you call me _____."

6. ASK THEM TO STOP. Say, "I know you have a choice, but I'd like you to think about my feelings and please stop calling me that. Will you do that for me?" Putting them in a position to say yes or no gives them some power back, which helps them feel better about being told they messed up.

7. ACCEPT THEIR APOLOGY. If they apologize, assume the best and accept it. It'll make you seem less threatening, which means they're less likely to attack you again. If they don't, you've said your piece and can move forward anyway.

Now. We're 100 percent aware that this is *not* what you see on social media. People behave badly, then they get dragged off the internet. We're talking about lasting change here, friends. Protecting yourself by preserving someone else's dignity.

There are definitely times when a public call-out is in order—when someone is violent or when someone is repeatedly bullying you. In those cases, you have to stop the harm the second it happens. But a one-time error in judgment is probably not the time to pull out your phone and start recording. Here's why:

• It might make the immediate situation unravel or get violent.
• It might not create lasting change.
• It might actually make you feel *worse* because, while they might deserve a good public dragging, it usually doesn't feel good to humiliate someone else.

A Final Word on Labels

It's important to remember all this before putting labels on other people too. Two cautions:

1. BE CAREFUL ABOUT MAKING ASSUMPTIONS BASED ON SOMEONE'S LABEL. Not everyone who is Muslim or introverted or gay or Black or an honor student looks, acts, or feels the same way. No single person is a representative for their entire label.

2. BE CAREFUL ABOUT USING A LABEL SOMEONE MIGHT NOT AGREE WITH. If you're not sure, ask them. And if you make a mistake about someone's labels, apologize and move on.

QUIZ TIME

Which Label Fits?

Yada, yada. Answer. Keep track.
(And remember: there are no wrong answers.)

1. **You and your friends see a person stranded by the side of the road with a flat tire, and you all decide to pull over. What do you do next?**

A. Change the tire. You know how to YouTube.

B. Use your phone to research solutions for them. Tow truck? AAA?

C. Take charge and organize your friends into a posse of helpers who offer snacks and call for help.

D. Comfort the person and offer them your best advice.

E. Stay with them until help arrives.

2. **Two of your friends are in an argument, and you feel stuck in the middle. What do you do?**

A. Jump in and help them figure it out.

B. Analyze the situation and provide logical advice if they ask for it.

C. Take a leadership role and decide who's right and wrong in the conversation.

D. Listen empathetically to both sides and offer emotional support.

E. Stay neutral, but be there for both friends if they need you.

3. **Your school is organizing a charity event benefiting an animal rescue. How do you help?**

A. Volunteer to set up tables and chairs.

B. Research and present information about the animal shelter at the event.

C. Organize the logistics and divide people into teams for snacks, drinks, and handling the dogs who will be available for adoption.

D. Connect with anyone who's adopted a pet, and share their stories with the leader.

E. Rally your friends to participate and show up to the charity event, cash in hand, to donate.

4. **Your classmate is struggling with their Spanish II notes. You:**

A. Offer to study together and share your Kahoot.

B. Explain verb conjugates in a way they understand.

C. Form a Spanish study group and take the lead in group discussions.

D. Text them daily encouragement and send them a link for Spanish tutoring.

E. Bring them study treats and help them stay focused while they study.

5. **Your friend is going through a tough time during their parents' divorce. How do you support them?**

A. Encourage them to face their emotions head on.

B. Share uplifting quotes that can inspire them to see through the pain to the hope that lies beyond.

C. Help them develop a plan to overcome the obstacles of having two homes.

D. Be a compassionate listener and offer a shoulder to lean on whenever they want.

E. Take them bowling, showing your unwavering friendship with distraction.

6. **Your school is hosting a talent show to benefit the arts department at your school, which the board is considering dropping. How do you participate?**

A. Showcase a talent like juggling or break dancing.

B. Offer to work through the schedule to coordinate the performances.

C. Take charge of organizing the ticket sales.

D. Sing a song that raises awareness for the cause.

E. Collaborate with friends on a group stunt performance.

7. **A new international student joins your class, and your vice principal gives you the task of showing them around. What do you do?**

A. Choose them for your team in PE and your review group in science class.

B. Share interesting facts about the clubs and classes available.

C. Introduce them to classmates as you walk them down the halls.

D. Express empathy and give them your Snap so they can message you if they're feeling lonely.

E. Invite them to join your lunch table and introduce them to your friends.

8. **Your school is organizing a community cleanup. How do you participate?**

A. Take a hands-on role, like picking up the trash or hauling yard waste.

B. Research and make the flyers so everyone knows the environmental impact you're making.

C. Lead a team and coordinate the cleanup efforts of two main roads.

D. Connect with community members to better understand their specific needs.

E. Sign up and ask all your friends to volunteer with you.

9. **Your English teacher just assigned you to groups to perform different acts of _Romeo and Juliet_. How do you contribute to the group?**

A. Stand up and perform Mercutio's lines to make them laugh.

B. Research the best people to assign to each role so you get an A.

C. Lead the group in planning, organizing, and delegating tasks.

D. Ensure everyone feels heard in group discussions instead of letting one person make all the decisions.

E. Bring in cookies as you all prepare to deliver your performance.

10. Your friend didn't make the soccer team. They're so disappointed that they're crying in the locker room. What do you do?

A. Show them a video of a great soccer player who failed repeatedly but ultimately achieved their goal.

B. Suggest practical steps to enhance their game play, like getting private lessons from someone who made it in exchange for tutoring.

C. Motivate them by offering to run practice drills with them after school.

D. Remind them of their strengths and let them know you care about them no matter what.

E. Assure them of your friendship and tell them you're there to help when they decide how they want to move forward.

Answers

IF YOU CHOSE MOSTLY A'S, YOU CAN CLAIM THIS LABEL: TRIED-AND-TRUE WARRIOR. You battle it out with confidence and fight through whatever you're given. You're mentally tough and can help others pull through when they're tired.

IF YOU CHOSE MOSTLY B'S, YOU CAN CLAIM THIS LABEL: INTELLIGENT KNOWL-EDGE SEEKER. You get to the facts and have no trouble sharing that information with others! You're willing to help with that stellar brain power of yours to make sure people get the facts they need to make informed decisions.

IF YOU CHOSE MOSTLY C'S, YOU CAN CLAIM THIS LABEL: DETERMINED LEADER. You're the person who steps up when everyone else is too nervous to try. You're great at managing projects and can help anyone achieve success with your incredible planning skills.

IF YOU CHOSE MOSTLY D'S, YOU CAN CLAIM THIS LABEL: COMPASSIONATE HELPER. You're empathetic and can see what others need to succeed. Your presence is calming, and you always try to be the best version of yourself so others have a light to follow in the dark.

IF YOU CHOSE MOSTLY E'S, YOU CAN CLAIM THIS LABEL: LOYAL FRIEND. You help other people believe in themselves, and they *love* to be around you. You're there for others no matter what, and you will make sure your friends achieve their biggest dreams, because you're there to help them through.

It's the Write Time

Make a list in your phone or on a piece of paper of five labels that make you feel good inside. Next to each one write down one action you can take to showcase that word in your everyday life. For example, if you choose "brave" as one of your words, maybe your action is: "Tell my dad that I want to try soccer instead of baseball," or "Sit with people who are nicer to me at lunch tomorrow." If you choose a religion as one of your words, maybe your action is to act on one of your religious beliefs, spend time in prayer, or visit someone who's sick or needs your help.

Call Me This, Not That Discussion
QUESTIONS

1. Have you ever gotten a nickname you really loved? How did you get it?

2. Tell a story about a time you called out someone or saw someone being called out for garbage behavior.

3. If you had to choose three positive labels for yourself, what would they be?

4. Discuss the benefits of calling someone *in* versus calling them *out*.

5. What are some assumptions people make about you based on a label you've given yourself? Do their assumptions fit who you are?

CHAPTER 8

I'M OKAY IN THIS SPACE

YOU EVER WALK INTO A STORE OR RESTAURANT AND HEAR A small voice in your head going, *Nah. This spot isn't for me.* The vibe is off, even if no one's looking at you funny, and you get that wormy kind of feeling that you're just not welcome.

It sucks. Places do exist that don't want teenagers in them, which is kinda rude if you ask us. Some people even *enjoy* kicking teenagers out of their spaces or banning them if parents aren't around. It's happened all over the country, from parks in California to malls and amusement parks in the Midwest and Northeast. Several of these owners have blamed social media stars and their obnoxious stunts for the restrictions. And yeah, obviously if a person is acting feral, throwing lettuce all over a Chipotle to get content for their YouTube channel, it isn't cool. But is the solution to restrict every teenagers' access to spaces they might enjoy? We think not.

However, we don't make the rules for the entire country, unfortunately. (If so, everyone would get a free kitten.) As it is, let's just make sure you know the kind of behavior most people expect in public spaces:

Act Like You've Been Somewhere 101

WHEN YOU'RE . . .	YOU'RE EXPECTED TO . . .
. . . at a sit-down restaurant	. . . keep your voice at a similar volume to others. . . . sit, eat your meal, then leave after you pay the bill.
. . . at school	. . . follow the rules. . . . keep yourself and others safe.

WHEN YOU'RE . . .	YOU'RE EXPECTED TO . . .
. . . at a funeral, vigil, or wake	. . . read the room. Some funerals are loud and filled with laughter. Others are somber. Match the energy. . . . respect others' feelings by offering condolences. Something like, "I'm so sorry for your loss" works well.
. . . at a wedding	. . . arrive early to be seated, or if you're running late, slip inside quietly. . . . go with the vibe. Some weddings are formal and refined, while others practically require breakdancing at midnight.
. . . in a religious service or ceremony	. . . respect the traditions. If you don't know what to do or say, ask someone who does. . . . stay quiet when the minister or religious leader is speaking, performing rituals, or completing rites unless others are speaking around you.
. . . at a fast-food restaurant	. . . order food, eat, then leave when you're done. . . . clean up after yourself.
. . . at a movie theater	. . . stay quiet, and keep your screen on low light if you have to text. . . . bring everything out, including trash, when the film is over.
. . . at an amusement park, arcade, trampoline park, playground, ski resort, and so on	. . . have fun. It's literally there for your enjoyment, and quiet isn't expected. Just don't break stuff, hurt people, make a mess you don't clean up, or cut lines.
. . . in a group	. . . think for yourself. In a group you can easily become part of "groupthink," where it's nearly impossible to stand up to bad decisions because different points of view are squashed.
. . . alone in a place that could be dangerous for you	. . . stay alert. Keep your headphones off, AirPods out, and eyes watchful. Your phone should stay in your hand or be easy to access.

STAYING SAFE IN SPACES

Sometimes a place doesn't feel welcoming because of someone else's stereotypes or bigotry. As a teen, Tess brought a guy into a place that wasn't welcoming to people of color, which she didn't realize until they asked them both to leave. She did and never went back. If the vibe is off, trust your instincts, and find a place that's safe.

But I Don't Go to a Lot of Places

Maybe you're more of a homebody, preferring to stay in after a long day at school. Your parents or other interested adults might gripe that you're on your phone or playing video games too much when you *are* home, but sociology says that you're probably not doing anything wrong; you might just be logging into your *third place*.

What's a third place? Think of it like this:

- **YOUR *FIRST PLACE* IS WHERE YOU LIVE.** It's the place you feel most comfortable. Where you snuggle up on your bed, eat lots of snacks, and store all your cool stuff.
- **YOUR *SECOND PLACE* IS LIKELY SCHOOL.** It's where you go most often when you're not at home.
- **YOUR *THIRD PLACE* IS YOUR RELAXATION SPOT.** It's the place you go to have fun, talk to friends, make connections, and let go of any pressure to be super productive. You might even make connections with new people in this space too.

Back in the day, teens would meet up with friends in third places like parks, roller rinks, dance clubs, arcades, malls, movie theaters, sporting events, houses of worship, or restaurants. And obviously, people still do. We're not all hermiting in our houses every second of the day. But if you don't get out much, or if you can't access some of those spaces as a teen, you might find the connection you need right there on your phone or video game console.

Bonus? You might not have to deal with some of the problems associated with public spaces.

How to Handle the Problems

Sooner or later you're gonna hit a snag when you're out in public. Whether it's a Karen yelling at you not to ride your bike on the literal bike path or a space that just doesn't have what you need to exist comfortably in it, problematic stuff can go down. So it's good to know what to do.

PROBLEM 1:
THE SPACE DOESN'T WORK FOR ME

Let's say you show up to an amusement park to ride the Underworld of Doom. You've been waiting *months* for it to open, and it's finally here! *But* you have diagnosed claustrophobia, and waiting in the coffin-sized hallways would make you panic more than the 90-degree drop. Do you leave and miss out on the shrieking shadow people? Never! You just have to make sure the space works for you, which involves . . . your voice.

Yep! We know, we know. If you're the kind of person who melts into goo at the thought of actually asking for something, this might hurt a wee bit. But even if it takes practice, telling people what you need is a superpower that can save relationships and even your life one day!

If you need a physical or
mental health accommodation:

Most places have adaptations for people with mental or physical needs. People with anxiety or ASD, for example, can often skip the lines at amusement parks. People with physical limitations might be directed to a ramp or given a chair, even if they're not available for others. If you need an accommodation to make the space work for you, here's what you could say:

1. "Hi! I'm Kate, and my doctor has diagnosed me with anxiety. Can I skip the line? Will you let my friend come with me so I'm not alone?"

2. "I have a sensory processing disorder. Is there a quieter place I can sit?"

3. "Hey, I'm Luis. As you can see, I'm in a wheelchair and need a ramp to get in the building. Where can I find that?"

4. "I have Sever's disease and my heels get really inflamed when we do mountain climbers, Coach. Can I do squats instead?"

If you need a different size:

Whether you need to go down in clothing or up in seatbelts, you're allowed to exist in the store, restaurant, or plane exactly as you are. It's perfectly okay to make the space work for you. Try this:

1. "Can I get a cup size down in this bra, please? If you don't have it in stock, do you have it online?"

2. "I'll take a table instead of a booth if you have one. If not, I'll wait."

3. "Hi, I need a seatbelt extender, because this airplane belt doesn't fit across my lap properly. Thank you!"

4. "Do you have a seat with a better view? I can't see over anyone's heads!"

PROBLEM 2:

SOMEONE DOESN'T WANT ME IN THE SPACE

Sometimes it's less about the space itself and more about the people in it.

If an adult is rude to you:

Let's say you're in a sandwich shop and the couple in the next booth keeps telling you to shut up because they say you're too loud. First: Ughhhhhhh. Second: What do you actually do? If you're truly living up to the expectations of the space and the adult isn't being violent, try one of these:

1. **"ARE YOU OKAY?"** This three-word response can actually shut down negativity by flipping the script on them. It shows concern, but it also suggests the problem is theirs, not yours.

2. **"SOUNDS LIKE YOU'RE HAVING A HARD DAY. HOPE IT GETS BETTER."** This is a power move, especially if they're recording you. It makes you seem calm and more mature than they are, and if anyone watches it back, it'll show how responsible you really are.

3. **"DID YOU MEAN TO SOUND RUDE? IF NOT, IT CAME OFF THAT WAY."** This is more of a call-out, but you're still not accusing them of anything.

It's important to remember that you're at a disadvantage in these situations. Adults will often give each other the benefit of the doubt and assume you're the one in the wrong just because you're a teen. Make sure you stay calm and *only* respond to adults who aren't acting aggressively. If you can't handle it, tell an employee that an adult is harassing you. Some adults think they can boss teenagers around for no reason, and arguing with them will just increase problems.

If an adult wants to kick you out of a space you're allowed to be in:

You might be just living your best life on your skateboard, rolling down the sidewalk, and a guy walks out of his house and demands you get out of his neighborhood. Or you're in the mall and a store clerk tells you to leave because you offend her. *heavy on the eyerolls* Try this:

1. **IGNORE THEM.** You don't have to listen to some random adult's demands unless they're a police officer or a shop owner in their own private business. If you trust that they're a safe adult, ignore and live your best life.

2. **INFORM THEM.** If you know you're in the right—you're not trespassing or restricted *and* they're an adult you'd consider to be safe—calmly tell them you're allowed to be there, *then* ignore them and live your best life.

3. **LEAVE.** Sometimes the safest thing to do is just dodge them for a while and circle back when they go away. Some adults are PROBLEMS and can react badly to teenagers telling them truths they don't want to hear.

From Tess to You

Don't give people the privilege of your presence if they don't want you there. If you feel unwelcome, take the gift of your company where it's appreciated.

Create Your Own Space

You won't always find welcoming spaces out there in the wide, wacky world, but you can definitely create space that's safe where you live. Here's how:

1. **PICK A SPOT.** Choose something that's just yours, even if you share a room. Maybe it's your bed or a corner of your room you can reserve for yourself.

2. **DECLUTTER IT.** Get rid of anything that stresses you out, whether that's trash, old clothes, electronics, or things that just don't suit you anymore.

3. **MAKE IT COZY!** Add pillows or blankets you love.

4. **DECORATE IT.** Use pictures, art, or objects that have special meaning to you.

5. **SET BOUNDARIES FOR YOUR USE OF YOUR SPACE.** Boundaries are limits you set on your own terms to prevent you from being taken advantage of, hurt, or manipulated. For example, a boundary you might set here could be: "I need space after school, so I'll be resting on my bed before homework. Will you please knock before you come in?"

6. **USE IT!** Whenever you need to feel pampered, head to your spot designed just for you.

A Final Word on Spaces

We want you to have space in this world that makes you feel loved and warm and welcome, virtual, in person, or otherwise. Everyone deserves that. If you're having trouble finding spaces where you feel like you belong, reach out to an adult who cares about you, and allow yourself to be vulnerable. Tell them how you feel. They can help you find or even create a spot where you're happy to go and others are over the moon that you're there.

XOXO

QUIZ TIME

What's Your Ideal Space?

Don't even think about skipping this one.

1. Which color palette speaks to your soul?

A. Soft pastels

B. Deep blue and muted gray

C. Vibrant green and sunshine yellow

D. Fire-engine red and midnight

E. Neon purple and techy blue

2. What's the temp?

A. Warm and toasty

B. Cool and crisp

C. Mild and breezy

D. Hot and sunshiney

E. Room temperature

3. What sound can you hear in the background?

A. The soft hum of a fan

B. Rain tapping on the window

C. Laughter and chatter

D. A ref whistle or a big band

E. Dings, zaps, and clicks

4. What's the vibe?

A. Cozy and safe

B. Calm and private

C. Social and lively

D. Competitive and high energy

E. Fast paced and thrilling

5. Where are you sitting?

A. On plush cushions and pillows

B. On a comfy chair by the window

C. On a picnic blanket in the grass

D. On the bleachers or stadium seats

E. In an ergonomic gaming chair

6. It smells like:

A. Freshly baked cookies

B. A crisp ocean breeze

C. Barbecue

D. Cut grass

E. An energy drink

7. When it comes to lighting, what's your pick?

A. Soft, warm fairy lights

B. A low-light lamp in the corner

C. Natural sunlight filtering through trees

D. Stadium floodlights at night

E. LED strip lights

8. Who are you listening to?

A. Morgan Wallen

B. Ice Spice

C. Chappell Roan

D. Drake

E. Tate McRae

9. What are you snacking on?

A. Hot cocoa with mini marshmallows

B. A bag of popcorn

C. Foot-long subs

D. Protein bars

E. Homemade nachos

10. Your ideal hang-out spot is incomplete without:

A. A great book

B. Good lighting

C. Group photos to capture the memories

D. Sports equipment

E. High-speed internet

Answers

IF YOU CHOSE MOSTLY A'S: You'd rather be snuggled up on your bed. Whether you're reading, scrolling, writing, daydreaming, or napping, you'd rather be solo in the coziest spot in the house.

IF YOU CHOSE MOSTLY B'S: You'd rather be FaceTiming friends on your phone in your room. You like to be at home, but you'd rather chat while you do it!

IF YOU CHOSE MOSTLY C'S: You'd rather be hanging outside with friends. Whether you're at a barbecue, a park, or a football game, you want to be in the great outdoors with a group of people who know you best.

IF YOU CHOSE MOSTLY D'S: You'd rather be at a sports practice or game with your best friend. You don't mind a little hard work! You'd rather play the game than sit on the sidelines, but even if you're not playing, you'd rather watch with a buddy at your side.

IF YOU CHOSE MOSTLY E'S: You'd rather be gaming with people online. You love the competition, the challenge, the music, and, most of all, the adrenaline rush of crushing the competition.

Tess's Extras

Tess's Three Steps for Faking Confidence When You Don't Feel It

In any space, you want to show up and show out for yourself, but that doesn't mean you're always going to *feel* the confidence you want to give off. Here's how to delude yourself into self-assurance so you feel good wherever you go.

STEP 1: CHANGE YOUR WORDS.

You don't try; you do. You're not a person who's *trying* to be confident. You *are* confident. When you change how you talk to yourself and others, you can kinda make yourself believe it.

STEP 2: PRETEND YOU'RE SOMEONE WHO *IS* CONFIDENT.

Take on a persona like Queen Bey does on stage with Sasha Fierce, and become the person who doesn't care what anyone else thinks of them in that space.

STEP 3: CHANGE YOUR BODY LANGUAGE.

Your own spine can help you become more self-assured. When you keep your shoulders back, head high, and heart forward, you will actually feel the confidence your body is giving off.

I'm Okay in This Space Discussion
QUESTIONS

1. Do you agree that social media can be a third place for teenagers? Why or why not?

2. If you could teleport to the absolute best space in the entire world, where would you go? Why?

3. If your friends are acting out-of-pocket in a coffee shop, what's a good way to get them to relax because the manager is giving you dirty looks?

4. Pretend a space isn't working for you for whatever reason. Practice a line you could say to someone in charge to make sure that it *does* work for you.

5. Design your ideal bedroom. What kind of bed are you sleeping in? What color are the walls? The bedding? The pillows? What does it smell like? What else is in the room?

CHAPTER 9

BUH-BYE FRENEMIES

WHY DO BULLIES EVEN EXIST?

It's a question for the ages. People have been battling frenemies, bullies, haters—whatever you want to call them—since people lived in caves. There was probably some guy named Glerg who bonked people on the heads with a stick and stole the raspberries they'd foraged because he could.

Who knows?

But as long as humans have existed, there are people out there who make it their full-time job to harass, bully, and generally make life miserable for others.

Bullying 101

True bullying, according to the U.S. Centers for Disease Control (CDC), is made up of these four things:

***1.* UNWANTED AGGRESSIVE BEHAVIOR:** If you ask someone to refer to you as fat, that's your business. Own your labels! If, however, someone body-shames you and slams your forehead into a desk because you look a certain way, that's bullying.

***2.* A POWER IMBALANCE:** If the little girl you're babysitting says you smell like a hot dog, that doesn't count. She's three, and chances are good you have more power than she does—depending on whether she's had a nap. If the prom king, however, tells everyone to call you "Hot Dog Water" and then they do for months, it's bullying.

***3.* REPETITION:** If the soccer captain laughs at your bad kick once and apologizes afterward, it's not great, but it's not really bullying. If the soccer captain constantly insults your skills in front of other people and doesn't seem pressed about it, then that's bullying.

4. HARMFUL EFFECTS: If you're physically, psychologically, socially, emotionally, or even educationally harmed by someone's consistent, aggressive behavior, then that's bullying.

Bullying legally overlaps with discrimination and harassment if someone messes with you because of your race, national origin, color, sex (including sexual orientation and gender identity), age, disability, or religion.

TYPES OF BULLYING

- **PHYSICAL BULLYING:** This is the obvious kind. Glerg bonks you on the head and steals your raspberries. Angelique throws spitballs in your hair when you sit in front of her in class. Suresh squeezes your belly when he walks past you.
- **VERBAL BULLYING:** This is when someone uses their voice to intimidate or hurt. Someone calls you Slender Man the entire year. Josh from your English class says you're too fat to fit into a desk. Your date says intimidating things that make you feel unsafe.
- **SOCIAL BULLYING:** This is the difficult one because it's hard to catch. It's also hard to correct because it's so sneaky. Three kids sit in the back of the classroom, looking at your friend and laughing. A rumor circulates that you're skinny because you're on drugs. Every time Javier sits at a table, the rest of the group sitting there gets up and leaves.
- **CYBER BULLYING:** This is the intimidation that shows up online. A frenemy gets in a fight with you, unfriends you on social media, and then makes TikToks about you. A kid screenshots a photo of you at a swim meet and makes that her profile picture. Ansley Snaps you hateful messages from one of her friend's accounts. You get FaceTimed by a group of people who laugh at you. Every time you join a group text, someone takes you off of it for no reason.

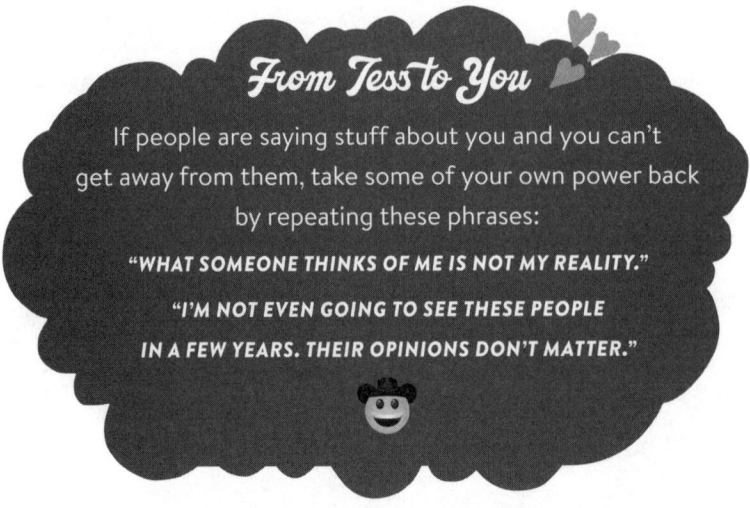

From Tess to You

If people are saying stuff about you and you can't get away from them, take some of your own power back by repeating these phrases:

"WHAT SOMEONE THINKS OF ME IS NOT MY REALITY."

"I'M NOT EVEN GOING TO SEE THESE PEOPLE IN A FEW YEARS. THEIR OPINIONS DON'T MATTER."

The Red Flags of Frenemies

Sometimes it's not all that clear whether you're being bullied. Sometimes the *worst* bullying can come from boyfriends, girlfriends, love interests, family members, and friends. (The word "frenemies" became a *thing* for a reason.)

So how can you tell if someone is a frenemy? You look for the red flags and the green flags:

• **RED FLAGS** are the behaviors that signal bullying, hatred, jealousy, and cruelty.

• **GREEN FLAGS** are the behaviors that signal friendship and love.

And listen, we get it. It *sounds* really easy, and you might be sure you've got it all figured out. Don't be friends with people who are crappy. Done.

But . . . in reality? The lines get blurry. Friends can morph into frenemies into toxic relationship partners whom you never want to see again in your life. It can take practice and paying attention to how people actually behave to figure all of this out. So let's take a peek at some examples of what to look out for in the chart on the facing page.

RED-FLAG BEHAVIOR	GREEN-FLAG BEHAVIOR
They only hang out with you if other people aren't around or available.	They save you a seat. They make room for you. They call, Snap, DM, and text you.
You find out they've been talking about you behind your back, and when you bring it up, they blame it on everyone else.	They never dismiss you or ignore you in a group and take your side if you're feeling picked on.
After hanging out with them, you feel exhausted, upset, zapped of energy, unsettled, or some other negative feeling.	You feel energized and happy after being with them.
They tell other people the things you've told them privately.	They keep your secrets unless it's in your best interest to share them.
They try to control what you say, how you act, or what you do. They choose the activities you do together.	They cooperate with you and get your opinion on things. They give as much as they receive.
They somehow get you to do things for them, but they rarely or never help you out when you need it.	They're willing to help you because they truly want you to succeed.
They don't listen when you say no and don't let you share your thoughts.	They listen whenever you speak.
When you get upset about their actions, they flip the script and make themselves the victim. They get angry, defensive, or cry, claiming that you're picking on them, trying to cause drama, or being uptight.	They accept blame and apologize when they've hurt you.
They get jealous of your accomplishments or try to one-up you whenever you bring up something good that's happening in your life.	They cheer for you when you've done a good job.
They gossip about other close friends of yours in front of you.	They don't gossip about your friends.
They are mean to you but qualify it as "just joking" or trying to give a "helpful critique."	They might tease or offer a critique, but it's never nasty.
They get jealous or angry when you spend time with other people.	They might feel a little jealous, but they give you space to be your own person.

Tess's Experience with Bullies

KELLY: Hey, wanna get into your trauma?

TESS: Haha.

KELLY: But seriously, should we talk about the bullies and frenemies you had in high school? How was it for you?

TESS: It was bad, y'all. Bad. There was this one girl who liked my boyfriend when I was in high school, and she would wait for me down the hallway and shove me into lockers and call me names. She taunted me throughout my ninth-, tenth-, and beginning of eleventh-grade years.

KELLY: *Wow.* That's really awful. I mean, get your own man.

TESS: Exactly. Basically, long story short, the guy—my high school boyfriend who I was in love with—became popular over one summer. He sang an Oasis song at a talent show, and everybody wanted him after that. So that meant everyone made fun of me. Like how could I possibly have gotten *him*?

KELLY: Oof. That had to hurt. But . . . tbh . . . Oasis? *That's* what did it for them?

TESS: Haha. Yeah. It ages us!

KELLY: It does!

TESS: Anyway, it really did hurt. This girl was behind the whole thing. And it just grew worse and was actually part of the reason I ended up dropping out of high school. I quit because of all the hate. I ended up getting my GED and actually finished before they all graduated, but . . . ya know. It hurt so much then, and I didn't know what else to do.

KELLY: No one stepped in?

TESS: No. He and I even went to the counselor and stuff and said, "Hey, this is going on," but they didn't care. They didn't do anything. Obviously, my life turned out the way it was supposed to, but back then it was really hard. Since then I've learned how to advocate for myself.

How to Stand Up for Yourself Even If No One Else Will

Maybe, like Tess, you've experienced bullying. It hurts, no matter what kind it is, and you should know what the heck to do about it if your friend list is bursting with red flags. One way you can help is by setting boundaries. Remember those? They're the limits you set that prevent you from being taken advantage of, hurt, or manipulated. Here's how to do it:

Step 1: **MAKE A LIST OF BEHAVIORS THAT NEED TO STOP.** On actual paper or in your Notes app, write down this stuff:

- **THINGS YOU WANT PEOPLE TO STOP DOING *AROUND* YOU.** For example, gossiping about other people, making fun of your parents, messing around when you're trying to focus, and so on.

- **THINGS YOU WANT PEOPLE TO STOP DOING *TO* YOU.** For example, taking your phone, DMing you at midnight, sitting on your lap, squeezing your stomach, yadda yadda.

- **THINGS YOU WANT PEOPLE TO STOP *SAYING* TO YOU.** For example, "teasing" that's actually insulting, calling you names, talking over you when you're trying to say something, you get the point.

Step 2: **WRITE A STATEMENT.** Choose one item from your list. Write a statement that tells the person to stop and explains how their behavior makes you feel. Like this:

- "I feel like garbage when you make fun of my mom. I want you to stop doing that around me."

- "It bothers me when you make comments about my body, especially after I've told you not to. Please quit."

- "It actually hurts when you knock me into the lockers. Don't touch me at all. Ever."

- "It makes me feel like crap when you talk over me. Like I'm not important. Please let me finish my sentence before you jump in."

Step 3: **ADD A CONSEQUENCE.** Take any of those statements you just wrote and add a consequence to the end that tells others what you will do if their behavior doesn't change. Like this:

- "I feel like garbage when you make fun of my mom. I want you to stop doing that around me. **I WON'T HANG OUT WITH YOU UNLESS IT ENDS.**"

- "It bothers me when you make comments about my body, especially after I've told you not to. Please quit. **I REALLY DON'T WANT TO STOP HANGING OUT WITH YOU, BUT I WILL IF IT HAPPENS AGAIN.**"

- "It actually hurts when you knock me into the lockers. Don't touch me at all. Ever. **I WILL GO TO THE PRINCIPAL, OUR COACH, THE LOCAL NEWS, AND THE COPS IF YOU KEEP IT UP.**"

- "It makes me feel like crap when you talk over me in the group. Like I'm not important. Please let me finish my sentence before you jump in. **I DON'T WANT THIS TO IMPACT OUR FRIENDSHIP, BUT I WILL HAVE TO TAKE A STEP BACK IF IT CONTINUES.**"

***Step 4*: DON'T FEEL GUILTY.** Lots of people push back when you require them to treat you with respect. They'll get annoyed, defensive, or even snippy. Welp? Practice saying, "Oh well!" If it doesn't fill your cup or bring you joy, it isn't right for you.

Setting a boundary protects you. It will make your good friendships even better because you help other people be *their* best selves around you. Bonus? It helps you shake free from toxic situations, because if others hate the boundary you've set up, they'll leave.

***Step 5*: BE CONSISTENT.** When people dislike a boundary, they'll kick against it. Your friend will talk right over you five minutes later or your bully will make a comment about your body the very next day. Boundaries only work if you enforce them.

Remind them of your boundary, and then activate your consequence. It's likely they'll respect you for standing up for yourself rather than taking the abuse over and over again. Even if they don't respect you or ever change, *you* will have. You'll emerge stronger, more confident, and less likely to be anxious or depressed.

FIVE THINGS TO SAY TO SHUT DOWN HATE

1. "I hope you find the love you clearly need."

2. "That's what you think. It's not my reality."

3. "Oh, it's so cute that you think that!"

4. "Bless your heart."

5. "I'm going to use my energy on things that make me happy rather than on what you just said. Bye!"

Oh Great.
Now I Don't Have Friends =(

Oops. You set some boundaries, and now there's a new, weird vibe with the girl you're talking to or tension between you and your best bud. Now what do you do on Friday night? Attend your neighbor's birthday party for Pickles, their teacup Yorkie?

Nah. (Although we resent the fact that we didn't get an invitation. We love dogs! And pickles!)

Anyway, you have options other than boredom, loneliness, or heartbreak, we solemnly swear. Here are just a few:

- **TRY SOMETHING NEW:** Now is the perfect time to try watercolor painting, video editing, cooking, skiing, beatboxing, or anything else that piques your interest. (Leave worrying about making mistakes behind. Those days are done.) Bonus? Fresh interests often bring fresh friendships!

- **FIND YOUR PEEPS:** Keep your eyes out for the green-flag people. Maybe it's Saadia, your lab partner who always gives you the good beaker, or Kate, who says hi every time she sees you at youth group. Grab their Snap or number. No one said the friends you made in first grade have to be your besties until you're ninety-seven. It's not a *rule*.

- **MAKE KINDNESS YOUR IDENTITY:** Be bold and do the wholesome thing you've been wanting to do. Stand up for that kid who gets called "whale" every single day of his life. Wash the dishes for your dad. Teach the kid next door how to shoot a basketball. Practicing kindness can literally change the trajectory of your life. Not only will you worry less about what the red-flag people are doing, but you'll also radiate confidence and attract the kind of people who also want to make the world shine.

A Final Word on Frenemies

Do you have someone in mind who waves so many red flags that you're actually shocked you've never gotten hit in the throat with them? Y'all, we get it. Sometimes it's hard to notice things that are right in front of our eyeballs when we genuinely care about another person. It's even harder when we love them and want them in our lives.

We just want you whole, healthy, and happy. We want you to live your life to the absolute fullest with people who celebrate you for the *amazing* person you are. And if that means dodging those red flags by stepping just a teeeensy bit farther away from them, then maybe it's time.

QUIZ TIME

Can You ID the Flags?

Okay, we're switching it up a little bit for this one. We want you to look for green-flag and red-flag behaviors. Remember, green flags are actions that show friendship or set boundaries. Red flags are the behaviors of people living in their toxic eras.

Hint: there may be both types in each scenario.

1. Jackson and Riley

"Hey! Can I come over?" Jackson asks Riley over FaceTime.

"Uh . . . no? It's eleven? On a Tuesday? My parents are in bed."

Jackson smiles one of Riley's favorite smiles. It's the mischievous one. Full of secrets. But it's also the one that brings out the nervous butterflies because Jackson can be unpredictable. "So?"

"*So?*" Riley smiles at him warily. "They'd literally kill me."

"Nah, they wouldn't. They'd never find out."

"I know you haven't met them yet, but I'm too young to die."

"I can be there in seven minutes. Six if I speed."

"Jackson—"

But he just hangs up. Riley repeatedly texts Jackson not to come, but a few minutes later Jackson parks his car down the street and jogs toward the house. Instantly annoyed, Riley texts Jackson that if he doesn't leave right now, there's zero communication happening between them tomorrow. He's crossed a line.

2. Jesse, Beau, and DeShawn

Beau sits down on a bench after track to change out of his shoes into slides. DeShawn sprawls out on the grass next to him while Jesse jogs up after finishing his cool-down.

"Coach was trippin' today," DeShawn says, wiping his hand down his face.

"I know. Felt like I was gonna puke on the last lap." Beau tucks his shoes into his bag and zips it up. "You heading out, or you wanna come with me and Jesse?"

"Where y'all goin'?"

"My house," Jesse says. "Grab somethin' to eat on the way probably too."

DeShawn blinks up at them past the burning sunlight high in the sky. "I don't know. Got stuff to do."

"Your choice," Beau says, standing up.

"Never mind. I'll come for a while. I gotta eat anyway."

"Cool. I'm gonna shower quick, and I'll meet y'all outside."

"Good," Jesse laughs. "You smell like a dead squirrel."

Beau sniffs his armpit, laughs, and heads to the locker room. "You know what? You're right. Be done in ten."

3. Emma, Javi, and Lanie

Lanie broke up with Javi three months ago and found out through Snap that Javi had started talking to Emma this past Monday.

She doesn't understand why, but the thought of Javi talking to her friend since fourth grade makes her sick to her stomach. It wasn't that she still liked Javi or anything. But she'd just started to get the ick for some reason and couldn't handle being around him anymore. But that doesn't mean she feels great that Emma is talking to him now. Especially since Emma knows how much Lanie used to care about him.

Lanie Snaps Emma later that night, but Emma leaves her on read. Hurt, Lanie sends her another Snap and then texts her a few minutes later when Emma doesn't respond again.

> "Are you actually talking to Javi?"

Emma doesn't reply, but a few minutes later Lanie gets a group FaceTime from Emma, Javi, and six other numbers she doesn't know. She picks up and can hear people talking, but they don't really say anything to her. She hears Emma's laugh and then everyone is laughing hysterically, and she doesn't know what's going on. She hangs up, confused. She texts Emma:

> "wtf"

Emma doesn't respond.

Lanie unfriends her on every platform and then starts a group text with her other friends, telling them what Emma is doing to her.

4. Aditi, Michael, and Michael's mom

Michael's mom made a video about how she line-dances with a prosthetic leg and posted it to YouTube. Again. She showed how she put on the prosthetic and everything. He asked her three weeks ago to stop making videos like that because half the kids in his class were following her purely to make fun of her for it. She told him that while she's truly sorry he's upset about it, she doesn't care if anyone makes fun of her, especially not high school freshmen at Hickory Hills High.

Aditi sends the video to Michael to let him know what some of the kids are saying in the comments. Michael tells Aditi he knows. He already saw all that and doesn't know what to do. Aditi says Michael is amazing and she's pretty sure he'll figure it out. He always does. She tells him that her cousin used to post pictures making fun of Aditi's acne and never took them down when she asked him to. Aditi tells Michael to just talk to his mom about it. See what happens.

Later, when Michael tells his mom about the comments, she ruffles his hair and says that every time the haters share her video, it just makes them money—money she can use to take him out to dinner. Besides, she feels good talking about her prosthetic leg.

Two hours later they sit at Texas Pete's Smokehouse, enjoying full racks of BBQ ribs, corn on the cob, loaded baked potatoes, and Oreo milkshakes. Michael decides not to care about his classmates' opinions of his mom's videos, recognizing that if she's happy, he can be too.

5. Paul, Claire, and Mei

Paul is an honor student who is in line to become the valedictorian. He's co-captain of the debate team and is just packing up his stuff from debate club when Claire, the other captain, stops him.

"Did you hear about Mei Zhang?"

Paul grabs his phone from the table. "No?"

With a glance over her shoulder at the door, she sidles up to Paul, a knowing smile on her face. "Well, she told me to keep it a secret but—she likes you."

Paul blushes all the way up his hairline. He looks down at his phone. "Knock it off, Claire."

"No, I'm serious," Claire says. "She'll be at the debate tomorrow night. She wants to *watch you in action*. She asked me if she had a *shot* with you."

Paul stuffs the rest of his things into his bag and zips it up. Fast. "You're being mean. Stop."

"Why don't you believe me?" Claire sticks her hands on her hips. "She literally just said that to me. Earlier today. At lunch."

But Paul knows better. Mei is the smartest person he's ever met. Very beautiful. So beautiful that it makes his head hurt. She's entire universes out of his league. "Leave it alone."

"Fine." Claire holds her hands up. "Don't believe me. But she said she's going."

Paul escapes before Claire can embarrass him further.

The next night Paul spots Mei in the audience during the debate. He studiously avoids looking at her so he can attempt to win. But he finds his eyes drifting to her over and over again as his team rapidly and succinctly annihilates their opponents. She catches him looking at her when he's closing and offers him a smile brighter than the whole sun.

After the debate Mei approaches Paul to congratulate him on the win and asks him if he wants to go to a nearby café to celebrate. Paul smiles and says he wishes he could, but the team is going out to dinner. He asks her to join them instead. Shyly, she agrees, but only if the rest of the team doesn't mind. They don't! So she tags along, chatting happily, and somehow, miraculously, Paul finds himself sitting next to the smartest, most beautiful girl on the planet, wondering how he's possibly gotten this lucky.

Answers

1. JACKSON AND RILEY

RED FLAGS: Jackson repeatedly ignores what Riley says. Jackson argues when Riley says not to come over and then comes over anyway.

GREEN FLAGS: Riley states clearly that Jackson cannot come over. They text Jackson that he needs to leave and give him the consequence if he doesn't.

2. JESSE, BEAU, AND DESHAWN

RED FLAGS: There aren't any. Jesse teases Beau, but it's good-natured teasing. They're clearly friends, and Beau laughs after Jesse says it. If it happened over and over again, and Beau felt hurt, that could become a red flag.

GREEN FLAGS: Beau asks DeShawn to come hang out with him and Jesse but doesn't apply pressure. Jesse welcomes DeShawn when Beau invites him to hang out with them.

3. EMMA, JAVI, AND LANIE

RED FLAGS: This whole thing is a red flag, basically. Lanie Snaps Emma to find out what's going on. Emma and Javi's group call is cruel. Emma ignoring Lanie's messages is cruel. Lanie reaching out repeatedly when she knows it won't be well received is problematic. Unfriending everyone, then texting her friends about the situation instead of Emma is also problematic.

GREEN FLAGS: Pretty much nothing done in this scenario is a green flag. What *should* have happened: When Lanie finds out, she should move on with her day. It doesn't concern her. Emma should respond to Lanie's messages. She doesn't need Lanie's permission to talk to Javi, of course, but a friend will at least check in with her and let her know what's happening, especially if she knows Lanie once cared about Javi. If Lanie doesn't accept that, it's on her.

4. ADITI, MICHAEL, AND MICHAEL'S MOM

RED FLAGS: Michael's classmates mocking his mom is a red flag. So is Aditi's cousin posting unwanted photos of her and not taking them down when she asks.

GREEN FLAGS: Aditi gives Michael a heads-up about his mom's video, knowing that Michael will be upset when he sees it. She offers him friendly advice. Michael also responds well and confides his feelings in her. Michael's mom acknowledges his feelings but sticks to her decision, as the videos are of her only, not Michael, showing that she will not let someone's opinion shape her life.

5. PAUL, CLAIRE, AND MEI

RED FLAGS: Mei confides in Claire, and Claire immediately tells her secret. Claire seems to want to create some chaos. Claire doesn't listen when Paul tells her to stop.

GREEN FLAGS: Paul tells Claire to stop repeatedly and leaves the room when she doesn't listen. Mei politely asks Paul out for coffee. Paul doesn't break plans with his team but invites her along instead. Mei agrees to come only if his other friends don't mind. The team welcomes her.

Draw It Out

Time to doodle! Get out some markers or crayons and a pencil. Get a sheet of paper, and fold it in half length-wise.

On the left side, draw a red flag at the top of the page. Now draw the name of the biggest red-flag person of your life, even if that's a bestie, love interest, casual acquaintance, or family member. Under their name draw a picture showing how their actions make you feel.

On the right side, draw a green flag at the top of the page. Write and decorate the name of a person who gives you all sorts of green-flag behaviors. Under their name, draw a picture that shows how their actions make you feel.

Then ask yourself who you'd rather spend your time with.

Buh-BYE Frenemies Discussion
QUESTIONS

1. What kind of bullying happens most at your school? Physical, verbal, social, or cyber?

2. What's a boundary you can set for yourself to minimize the damage from a red-flag frenemy?

3. If most of the people in your life are more frenemy than green-flag friends, how can you get more of the good kind of friends? Where can you find them?

4. Describe how your best friend or a close family member treats you that lets you know they care about you.

5. What's one of the best comments you've ever gotten on social media? How did it make you feel?

CHAPTER 10

LET'S GET SOCIAL

KELLY: What's your favorite social media app?

TESS: TikTok, for sure. It's fun and doesn't feel like a lot of pressure. I learn a lot too. Weird stuff I never thought I'd need, but here I am at two o'clock on a Thursday, learning how to rope a steer.

KELLY: Something everyone needs.

TESS: Absolutely. Haha.

KELLY: Do you post a lot?

TESS: Right now I'm posting about two times a week on Instagram and daily on TikTok, but I probably need to post more on IG for sure.

KELLY: Why?

TESS: Well, in my industry, opportunity is everything, and social media gives me that. I mean, I got the *Cosmo* cover because of posting on social media.

KELLY: Really?! TELL ME EVERYTHING.

TESS: Haha! So I met the editor of *Cosmo* at an event in London where I was speaking on a panel. Two days later she was in my DMs, asking if I'd like to be on the cover. I had to take it to my team and ask them if it was legit. They said, "Tess, no one ever jokes about a *Cosmo* cover."

KELLY: Oh, in fact they do not.

TESS: Right? It was such a big deal to me. I cried!

KELLY: I bet you did! And all because you put yourself out there.

TESS: Exactly, though sometimes I do have to remind myself to take breaks if it starts messing with my mental health.

KELLY: I mean, smart, but it sucks that it can affect you like that. I guess it does that to *all* of us from time to time, though. How does it impact you?

TESS: Oh, just your standard trolling. Bullying. And if it gets to be too much, I'm gone. If I'm not on social, they can't find me, right? And also just making comparisons to other people. I have to remind myself that some people don't even start being successful until their fifties or sixties, so why am I worrying about whether one of my posts went viral or not? It can be difficult to get out of your own head sometimes, so if I find myself in that space, I just log off.

KELLY: Who knew that when social media got started, taking breaks would be a thing we had to do?

TESS: Not me, that's for sure. Not back when I was on LiveJournal, which was before MySpace.

KELLY: Then you went to Facebook?

TESS: Yeah, I actually made a Facebook page on a dare! My friend Krystal and I had just gotten our first modeling gigs, and she joked that we should get a fan page started on Facebook. I told her that no one would ever follow me except, like, two friends and my family, but I ended up doing it anyway in 2010.

KELLY: And what happened?

TESS: My account blew up! It's where I got most of my early followers.

KELLY: And now millions follow you on every platform.

TESS: It still blows my mind!

Social Media: How It Started

It's tough to pinpoint the exact start of social media, but the 1990s is really when the idea of a virtual community arose. Before then it just wasn't a thing. People called each other on literal house telephones with physical cords and trusted that their friends were going to show up at the movie theater at 6:30 p.m. like they'd promised.

Seems totally strange now, but it's true!

A TIMELINE OF DEVELOPMENT:

- 1995: America Online (AOL) chatrooms went live.
- 1997: First social networking sites Bolt and Six Degrees began.
- 1998–1999: Social blogging sites Open Diary and LiveJournal
- 2003: LinkedIn and MySpace
- 2004: Facebook
- 2005: YouTube and Reddit
- 2006: Twitter (now X)
- 2007: Tumblr
- 2009: WhatsApp
- 2010: Pinterest and Instagram
- 2011: Snapchat
- 2013: Telegram
- 2014: Musical.ly
- 2015: Discord
- 2017: TikTok

There are dozens more that came and went, but these are most of the majors.

Social Media: How It's Going

Today there are about 5.85 billion social media users, and most of us spend roughly two and a half hours a day on social platforms, though some of us *cough* are on it *waaaay* more than that. And although your grandma and her bestie might be posting daily on Facebook—making it the most popular social media site in the world—y'all tend to prefer YouTube, followed by TikTok, Snapchat, then Instagram (though we're betting we didn't have to tell you that).

WHY IS SOCIAL MEDIA SO POPULAR?

People like to get all screechy about you being addicted to social media, but *are* we addicted? Is that actually true? Dr. Nika Douvikas, our pediatrician consultant, says it *can* be addicting.

Getting that new like or follow activates the reward system in our brains by dosing us with *dopamine*, a neurotransmitter called the "feel-good" hormone. Dopamine gives us a jolt of feel-good vibes after doing stuff like chomping on mouth-watering food, finishing a tough workout, or having a spectacular convo with a friend.

Orrrrrr getting a like, share, or comment on a social media post. =|

Here's the thing: our silly-wickle brains can't tell the difference between "*omg ily girly pop*" and a regular conversation, so it gives us a hit of dopamine every time we get a notification. Why? The old noggin wants to make sure we keep talking because throughout history having a friend was the number one way to fight off guys like Glerg who wanted to steal your raspberries. There's power in a pack!

The problem? When you don't get a like and don't get that lil' dopamine surge, you can spiral downward into not-so-fun things like anxiety and depression. Ugh.

THREE UPSIDES OF SOCIAL MEDIA

Despite the chokehold social media has on our brains, there are some top-tier benefits of downloading an app and logging in from time to time:

1. **CONNECTION:** You might not be able to meet up with Tony and his new boyfriend for burgers at Steak 'n Shake, but you can get on Snap and say hi. You can also send a picture to your mom showing off the shoes you saw on Instagram (with the link *wink wink*), text a video to your brother at college, join a study chat for Bio, and play video games with a guy from New Zealand at 3:00 a.m. when you're supposed to be sleeping.

2. **CREATIVITY:** You don't take piano lessons anymore after that run-in with your teacher (sorry about your cat, Ms. Rhonda), but you just taught yourself Coldplay's "The Scientist" after watching a streamer. Last week you YouTubed how to clear the cache on your computer, install a bidet on your toilet, make a Philly cheesesteak, and draw a realistic tiger shark.

3. **CONVENIENCE:** Your teachers post all their assignments in Canvas. Your gymnastics coach started a GroupMe for practice. Your school updates their X, Instagram, and Facebook accounts with deadline reminders. You joined a Facebook group to try to get recruited for baseball. You see that Jeremy paid Olivia $20 on Venmo, and oh shoot, you still owe her.

THREE DOWNSIDES OF SOCIAL MEDIA

Social media isn't all Philly cheesesteak recipes, is it? Nope. It can be a sack of rotting fish carcasses too, as we're sure you know. Some days we wonder if it's worth it when this stuff exists:

1. **BULLYING:** You get trolled by randos when you post a picture of yourself in a political party T-shirt. Your Instagram Reel about your cat gets sent around at school as an example of what not to do. Some girl makes a TikTok of you asking for more cream cheese in a bagel shop, and you become known as "Cream Cheese Playa" on Snap.

2. **COMPARISON:** Your teeth aren't as white as Amara's. Your back isn't as strong as Mason's. Your posts only get two hundred views, and Nixon's get two thousand. Your pictures aren't as aesthetic as Emily's, and your family doesn't go on all the spectacular vacations that Darian's family does. Everyone else has more money, more clout, better hair, and leaner muscle mass, and you're a dumpy potato no one likes.

3. **FAKERY:** A cute guy slides into your DMs, but when you meet up with him at the mall, he's at least thirty-seven and you're scared of him. Janie acts like your friend on Snap and a stranger in person. You know that every one of Kenji's selfies is altered with Facetune.

Social media has its benefits, sure, but the downsides can sometimes feel heavy. Dr. Patrice Berry, our child psychologist consultant, says that although it's normal to compare yourself to others, comparison is a thief of joy. It can make you feel bad about yourself—or good about yourself for a bad reason.

She says to remember that things always look shinier when you see them from the outside. Darian's family might fight every time they travel. Amara might use a filter for her teeth. Kenji is faking his entire face! You just don't know what's real, so it's best not to use it as a measure of your self-worth.

MORE PEOPLE, MORE PROBLEMS

If Trinity makes a nasty comment about your friend in a group chat, take care of the problem yourself. Tell Trinity not to message you stuff like that anymore. If you screenshot it and send it to your friends who all pile on Trinity, you've taken a minor problem and ballooned it into a major one. End it with you. The only time you need to share is if someone is a danger to themselves or others.

A Guide for Protecting Your Mental Health

All right, so it isn't always easy to hike the winding, rocky path of social media, so here's a little guide to make sure your mental health is *all* good as you scroll:

FOLLOW THE PATH: Interact with accounts that:

- Have good energy
  - Green-flag friends who care about you
  - Entertainers you admire
  - Mental health advocacy
  - Issues you care about
- Can positively impact your future
  - Colleges/trade schools/your school
  - Careers
  - Volunteering opportunities
- Give you creative ideas
  - Artists
  - Personal interest groups
  - Skill-building accounts

WATCH YOUR STEP: Be wary of accounts that:

- Make promises
  - Health accounts that guarantee quick change
  - Self-improvement accounts that require a subscription or purchase
- You don't know in real life
  - Friends of friends
  - Anyone sliding into your DMs without an introduction
- Take up a lot of time
  - Constant pressure to respond
  - Constant distraction

TURN AROUND: Stop interacting with accounts that:

- Give you negative feelings
  - Shame you
  - Sicken or sadden you
  - Make you feel jealous or unloved

- Exploit others for views
  - Harm others
  - Make fun of others
  - Are intrusive in other people's spaces
- Make you feel uncomfortable or unsafe
  - Break your boundaries
  - Send you content, photos, or videos you don't like
  - Harass or bully you

From Tess to You

It's been said a dozen times, but it's good to remember: social media shows you the highlight reel of people's lives, not their day-to-day. For every glam event I show online, there are a thousand more photos I could take cleaning the house. Social media is *not* reality. Keep that in mind before you tie your self-worth to someone else's posts.

We're on a Break

Let's say you've watched one too many YouTube videos, have followed and unfollowed people on Instagram so many times that you can't see straight, and are bored to weeping with Snap. I mean, how many ceiling pictures can you even see in a day before your brain turns to oatmeal and glops out of your ears?

But how do you take a break without losing your friends? Let's head back a few decades, and we'll show ya.

PRETEND IT'S THE '90S TO CONNECT WITH FRIENDS	PRETEND IT'S THE '60S TO CONNECT WITH FAMILY
Go glo-bowling.	Ask for a family dinner at the table once a week.
Rollerblade.	Download some conversation starters and ask questions like: "If you could invite one famous person to dinner, who would it be and why?"
Attend a bonfire and make s'mores (or host one if you have a big backyard).	Host a family and friends game night where everyone gets to invite one person they like.
Have a sleepover and watch old-school movies.	Learn how to grow a container garden or make sourdough bread with a family member.
Go to an arcade.	Teach everyone a new card game and bet money/chores/family clout on it.

From Tess to You

One of my favorite ways to connect offline is with sleepovers. Don't get me wrong, I also love going out dancing and listening to music. But I *love* a night in too. Uno tears families apart, but it's so much fun. My friends and family love piling blankets in the living room, playing Connect 4 and Guess Who, and making up our own rules as we go.

A Final Word on Getting Social

Let's face it. We're probably not going to stop watching YouTube videos or fishing for likes with videos of our dogs rolling around in the mud. But . . . we can manage how social media affects our life, Dr. Berry says. It just takes some shifts in how we think about things.

- **IF YOU'RE HAVING A BAD DAY, SHARE IT WITH YOUR CLOSE INNER CIRCLE ONLY.** The world doesn't know you, and their feedback can make your day worse. Your inner circle loves you and can give you the support you need. Tell them and *only* them. Not everything in your life is content.

- **RESPOND INTELLIGENTLY INSTEAD OF REACTING TO NEGATIVE COMMENTS.** If some rando comments negatively about your legs in your new shorts, instead of clapping back about the size of their forehead or something, you could respond with, "Please don't comment on my body. Thanks!" Some people do things just to watch your head explode. But when you go off, you might not be staying true to who you are and the values you believe in. Plus, you could make your whole day worse by opening up the door for a longer conversation with even more hurt.

- **UNDERSTAND THAT YOU WON'T ALWAYS GET THINGS RIGHT.** A friend might make a comment online, and you might interpret it differently from how they meant it. You're not actually in their brain, right? Ask yourself if there's even a fingernail of possibility that you didn't understand what they meant, and then reach out to them privately if you want clarification.

- **DON'T GO BACK AND FORTH.** It's not productive or worth it to argue online. Sometimes you get caught up, wanting to fight every battle, but there are some fights that shift your focus away from your own goals. Say to heck with it, and log off.

- **ASK YOURSELF THIS: WHO WILL I ALLOW TO BOTHER ME?** If someone doesn't know you—or doesn't know the *real* you—don't let them occupy any space in your mind. You have better things to think about, like how far away the nearest volcano is or which microwave popcorn tastes best. Literally anything other than clowns clowning on your posts.

- **TAKE BREAKS.** If social media is draining your downtime, preventing you from achieving the really boss-like things you want to achieve or making you feel bad about yourself or others, guess what? It might be time to set some limits. If you can't do it yourself, ask someone who loves you to help.

QUIZ TIME

Which Social App Can't You Live Without?

In case you forgot: answer each question,
and keep track of the letters you choose.

1. You only get three colors, and they are:

A. Black, red, and white

B. Magenta, purple, and orange

C. Turquoise, hot pink, and black

D. Yellow, black, and white

E. Light green, dark green, and white

2. You can only choose one:

A. Tutorials on getting things done

B. An aesthetic photo diary

C. Short comedy sketches

D. Quick snaps of my ceiling

E. Group chats with my best friends

3. In your room you're going for this lighting vibe:

A. Studio lighting

B. Golden-hour sunlight

C. Disco ball reflections

D. Flashlight in the dark

E. Subtle candlelight

4. Choose an emoji:

A. 🎬

B. 📷

C. 🤼

D. 👴

E. 🔋

5. This flower is growing in a pot on your front porch:

A. Sunflower

B. Rose

C. Orchid

D. Snapdragon

E. Lily

6. Your phone has this pulled up right now:

A. A long-form tutorial teaching you how to check your oil

B. A feed of muted rose tones

C. A video of a guy parasailing

D. A pic of your pet snake, Ralph

E. A text from your boyfriend, Peter Parker

7. This is blasting through your AirPods:

A. A podcast with three people laughing

B. Folk music complete with twangy guitar

C. Funky pop music

D. The laugh track to a YouTube video

E. Your mom going *awf* in a voice message

8. After school your grandma took you to this (and you wanted to go):

A. A woodworking studio

B. A history museum

C. A disco dance club

D. An amusement park to ride the Underworld of Doom

E. A cozy coffee shop

9. Your superhero power is:

A. Reading other people's minds

B. Photographic memory

C. Time manipulation

D. Invisibility

E. Mind control

10. You've just earned your 100 millionth follower for:

A. Hosting tutorials of bicycle tricks

B. Posting color-coordinated aesthetic photos of books

C. Hosting challenges and donating the money to the homeless

D. Posting videos of your DMs

E. Podcasting about sports

Answers

IF YOU CHOSE MOSTLY A'S: You're a YouTube fan. You'll take the tutorials, shorts, and videos that entertain and inform over anything else.

IF YOU CHOSE MOSTLY B'S: You're an Instagram fan. You love beautiful things, artistic expression, and following your close friends and celebrities to stay in the know.

IF YOU CHOSE MOSTLY C'S: You're a TikTok fan. You like short, quick snippets to watch and make between running to class and waiting for your ride.

IF YOU CHOSE MOSTLY D'S: You're a Snapchat fan. You love connecting with your friends, watching short videos, and sending DMs and group chats that aren't permanent.

IF YOU CHOSE MOSTLY E'S: You're a WhatsApp (or other texting app) fan. You can skip the videos and pics because you're more interested in connecting with your friends in real time.

Tess's Extras

Tess's Six Tips for Using Social Media Thoughtfully

1. **UNFRIEND FRENEMIES.** You know who they are. They're the people who never engage with your page or try to connect even though they're literally stalking your content. You can change that with the click of a button. BYE.

2. CONNECT WITH GOOD FRIENDS. Connect with the people who want to cheer you on in all stages of your life, not just when you're doing well. The real friends stay when it's hard.

3. ADD IN THE FUN. It doesn't have to be all serious causes on your FYP, though those are important. Follow stuff that makes you laugh. We aren't saying turtles in hats are therapy, but . . . we're not *not* saying that.

4. FOLLOW PEOPLE OUTSIDE OF YOUR CIRCLE. You can learn outside of school. Strange, we know. But watching experts do their thing online is *amazing*. Take virtual guitar lessons from YouTube. Learn how to dance the bachata on TikTok. DO IT.

5. TRAVEL VIRTUALLY. Follow Bavarian bakers, Filipino dance artists, and Kenyan florists to expand your horizons without the need for a passport.

6. BE YOURSELF. Who you are is uniquely good. Social media sometimes tries to make you morph into what's popular, but being yourself is always on trend!

Let's Get Social Discussion
QUESTIONS

1. If you could only be on one social media app for the next ten years, what would you choose?

2. Discuss a time when social media was literally the worst thing to ever happen to you or someone you know.

3. You're a social media star with 100 million followers. How did you become famous? What are the downsides of your media fame?

4. Which are the three funniest accounts on YouTube? What are the three most inspiring on Instagram or TikTok?

5. If you were a teenager in the 1980s or 1990s without social media, do you think your life would be better or worse?

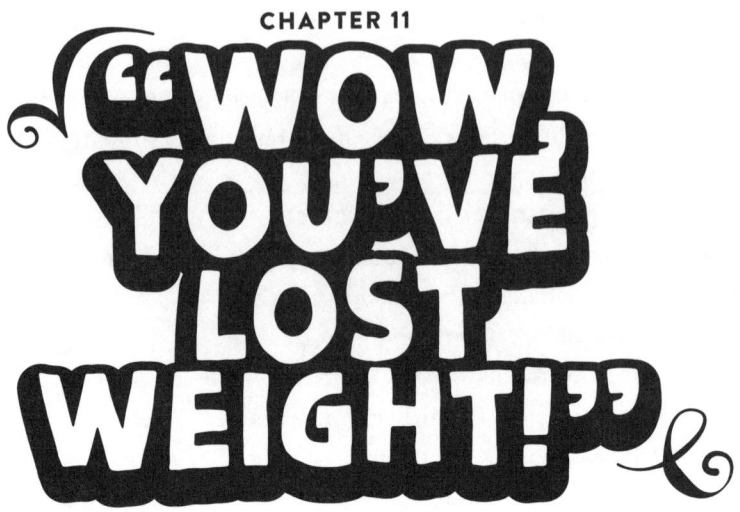

CHAPTER 11

"WOW, YOU'VE LOST WEIGHT!"

O**N TUESDAY, CHLOE WOKE UP FORTY MINUTES LATE, BUT IT** was exam week, so she didn't want to skip. She quickly got dressed, brushed her teeth, threw her white-blonde hair into a clip, and went to school, sliding into her seat a second before the bell rang.

At the end of the day, as she was waiting for her ride, Aiden, the guy who sits next to her in English, asked her something about her eyebrows.

"Hunh?" Chloe looked up from her phone.

"Your eyebrows." He pointed to his own.

Confused, Chloe ran a finger over her right brow. *What was wrong with them? What did he mean?*

"They're so blonde," he explained.

Chloe's cheeks grew hot as she got it. Her white-blonde hair had been passed down from great-grandparents born in Norway, which meant that unless she wore mascara and used a brow pencil, her eyelashes and eyebrows were nearly invisible. She'd missed her entire makeup routine earlier because she'd been running late.

"Um—" she started, but she let her explanation die in her throat as she thought back to second grade. How the kids had called her "Ghost Girl" until her teacher had lectured them about bullying. How she'd felt like she stuck out like a bleach spot in the colorful fabric of her class picture. How her mom had finally, *finally* let her start wearing mascara and eyebrow pencil in sixth grade and then the teasing died down. But now, one missed day of makeup, and she was right back to that horrible feeling of loneliness.

"Just my natural brows," she said quietly as her ride pulled up. She turned away so he couldn't see her embarrassment and then sprinted like a gazelle toward the car.

Aiden was immediately sorry he'd opened his big, stupid mouth, a problem he was trying (and repeatedly failing, if his mom was right) to fix.

"Chloe!" he called after her. "I didn't mean it like that. I'm sorry! I like them! They're pretty!"

But he could tell it didn't make her feel any better, and he groaned in frustration as she slammed the door and rode away. He wanted to *kick* himself. He'd finally gotten up the courage to talk to Chloe, the hottest girl in the entire school, and he'd messed it up.

"Couldn't think of anything to talk about besides her eyebrows, you idiot?" he scoffed at himself as he ran to catch the bus. He loved her soft eyelashes and pretty hair and thought everything about her was perfect. Why hadn't he said *that* instead of yammering on about her *eyebrows*? He slumped into a seat after he got on the bus, brooding about his mistake the entire ride home.

Those Body Comments

Aiden isn't the only one sticking his foot in his mouth when it comes to stuff like this. Look, he didn't even *mean* anything negative when he said it, right? He was trying to talk to her! But Chloe received it that way, no matter what his intention was. A person's intention is not always equal to another's reception, and it all gets *super* muddy when it comes to commenting on a person's body.

These are representative of the types of comments that show up on Tess's social media. You'll notice—*ahem*—that some of these are meant to be positive and some are very obviously meant to be negative:

• You are so stunning! I wish I could be like youuuuu.

• I'm not body shaming in any way shape or form but she looks so unhealthy. How can any of you people support this? She's obese.

• what a beautiful angel

• I have a real question and I'm not trying to be mean . . . Do you eat healthy and exercise at all? Just wondering. =(

• This is all so unattractive. Gross.

• Girl!!!!!!! I love your hair!!!! You remind me of Ginger Spice!!!!!

- Ughh. Always glowing. Always gorgeous. Slay. ✦⁺
- so we're all just celebrating an eating disorder—cool

We know you've seen comments like this on people's posts. Maybe even on your own. The negative ones can be hard to read (and even harder to receive), but even the ones intended to be positive can end up feeling negative if there's pressure associated with it. Like if my hair looks good online but not in person, do I still look good? If I'm a different size in person than my latest picture, will people call me fake? Ugh. It's a lot. Which begs us to ask the question: *Why are we commenting on people's bodies at all?*

From Tess to You

There are a zillion compliments to give that have nothing to do with someone's body. Try these:

"YOU'RE A GREAT PERSON. DID YOU KNOW THAT? YOU ARE."

"I LOVE YOUR BACKPACK."

"YOUR POSITIVE ENERGY IS GIVING ME LIFE."

"I FEEL SAFE AROUND YOU."

"WHY DO YOU ALWAYS COOK THE BEST FOOD?"

"YOU SEEM LIKE A GOOD DUDE."

"I'D LOVE TO HANG OUT WITH YOU MORE. YOU'RE SO FUN!"

"HOW ARE YOU THIS SMART, THOUGH?"

"YOU SLAYED THAT EXAM."

"YOU ARE SO FUNNY."

"ANYONE EVER TELL YOU THAT YOU GIVE GREAT ADVICE?"

When Words Are a Kick in the Shin

Some people, like our shy boy Aiden, have zero clue that they're making someone uncomfortable by commenting on their hair, skin, body size, or even eyebrows. It's worse online because you don't have the benefit of body language to help you express yourself. And if you *do* decide to compliment someone's body pic on Instagram or something, you could run into this kinda trouble:

1. You might give a compliment to someone who absolutely does not want your input.

2. You might say something that comes off completely wrong, even if you *do* know a person wants your flattery, because it's hard to get a compliment right when it's just a few words long.

3. You could accidentally *really hurt someone* without intending to because you don't know a person's history, their self-doubts, and their body image.

Social media *realllllllly* impacts how we think about ourselves. We can make comparisons that can give us a crappy body image. In fact, there was a study done in Boston with 1,480 people from the ages of thirteen to seventeen. The researchers asked them how social media made them feel about their bodies, and almost half (nearly 700!) said it made them feel worse than before they had social media accounts. Boo. =(

So let's be sure we're not contributing to any of that with what we say. Here are some common intrusive comments to avoid, whether you're online or in person:

BODY TOPIC	COMMENTS AND QUESTIONS TO AVOID
Skin color	• What *are* you? • Why are you so pale? • Oooh, your skin is just the right shade of tan.
Disability	• You're so inspirational! • Why are you in a wheelchair? • Hope they find a cure soon.
Height	• You're so lucky you're tall. • Do you play basketball? • We stan a short king.
Hand or foot size	• You know what they say about guys with big hands, don't ya? • You have little baby hands. • Those shoes look like canoes!
Hair	• Your hair looks so exotic. • Is that your real hair? • I'm so glad I don't have to spend that much time on my hair.
Body size	• Wow, you're a monster, man! • Babes, you should eat. You're looking skinny. • You look so good! I can tell you've lost weight.
Gender expression	• Are you a boy or a girl? • Why not just say you're the gender you were born with? • Which bathroom do you use?

You might have questions, or you might, like Aiden, have *feelings* and want to pay someone a compliment. Before you do, the rule of thumb is to *do no harm.* You can't hurt someone's feelings about their body if you don't comment on it at all. And if you're just curious, get to know the person, so maybe they'll feel comfortable answering any questions down the line.

BUT I'M THE ONE
GETTING THE BODY COMMENTS

Sometimes you're Aiden, sticking your foot in your mouth, and sometimes you're Chloe, wishing people would stop yapping at you about your biggest insecurity. How do you shut it down if people ask you questions, make comments, or give you compliments you don't want?

TEN RESPONSES THAT REDIRECT THE CONVO

There might be times when you want to let people know not to make comments on your body, but you feel aggressive drawing a hard line. First, to be clear, a boundary is not aggressive. It might *feel* aggressive if you've never set one before, and it might be *perceived* that way if the recipient has never gotten one before. But it isn't.

If you don't want to set a boundary, though, because the person is a frenemy, your boss at the coffee shop, that new classmate Lola, your Aunt Irene, or lemonpie5829 online—none of whom you feel safe confronting—choose redirection. You can state how you feel and then redirect with a question, flattery, or the introduction of another person. Here are a few examples:

1. Thanks, but I don't like compliments on my skin color. It feels weird. Nice profile pic, btw!

2. Can we please change the subject? How's your new dog? She's really cute.

3. Ugh, talking about my weight is so boring. Let's talk about you. What concert did you just go to? Drake?

4. My shoe size doesn't feel relevant to our Hannukah celebration, does it? Bubbe, can I help with anything in the kitchen?

5. I'd love it if you never mentioned my crooked teeth again. @tessholliday—can't wait to read your new book!

6. My disability isn't curable, but I appreciate you rooting for my general health anyway. You're so sweet!

7. I prefer not to talk about that with people I don't know well. Hey Jess, get in here. Have you met Anton?

8. I don't talk about personal things online, but thanks for the engagement on my post. You seem great. =)

9. Let's talk about literally anything besides the keto diet. You mentioned your new yoga pants. How do you like the brand?

10. Google is free if you're curious about hair like mine. In other news, I like those kicks.

TEN RESPONSES THAT HELP YOU STAND YOUR GROUND

Sometimes you want to tell someone that not only do you want them to stop talking about your body but you also want them to know *why they should stop*. Your aim is to both inform them and stop the behavior. When that happens, here are a few things you can say:

1. Someone's weight loss isn't something to compliment. I *think* you meant to compliment how hard I've been working at the gym. In that case, thanks! But to be clear, I'm not in charge of how my body responds to any of the exercises I'm doing. I'm only in charge of the choices I make as I take care of myself.

2. I'm offended by the comment about my hair. It makes me feel like I'm being *othered*, a concept you can look up if you don't want to do that again.

3. Please educate yourself on the topic of BMI. I'm focused on what my body can do rather than how it looks. I will not talk about it anymore with you.

4. Asking questions about my gender is an invasion of my privacy. My body parts are my business. Period.

5. Being called a monster or "hoss" isn't the compliment you think it is. It makes me self-conscious. Please stop.

6. Even when you're joking, the comments about the shape of my eyes really hurt. They bring up a lot of trauma. Did you know you were hurting me?

7. Please don't comment on my weight or anyone else's weight ever again. It's intrusive and can hurt people who might have body image issues.

8. It doesn't make me feel good when all our conversations end up being centered on my disability. Think of another topic, or I'll need to leave.

9. My ethnicity has nothing to do with you, and I'm not interested in discussing it with you.

10. I feel really uncomfortable when you talk about my body. It sounds creepy, and if you don't stop, I'll talk to my parents about it.

SHOULD I ANSWER THE QUESTION OR NOT?

A lady at Starbucks asks you a question or makes a comment that feels intrusive. Before you respond, check in with yourself:

• Do you have the emotional energy to deal with it?

• Do you *want* to talk about it?

If your answer is no, it's okay to simply say, "I don't want to talk about it right now," and leave the conversation.

A Final Word on Body Commentary

Chloe's eyebrow issue might seem small to some people, but to her, as a freshman in high school, it's everything. It's the ghost in her past that haunts her. Does that sound familiar? Is there anything about your body that you'd change if you could? A part of yourself that's bothered you forever? Many of us have *something*.

Our goal is that you walk away from this book knowing that even if you've got beef with your hair, your size, your eye color, your whatever, that it could be just the thing someone else admires about you. It could also be something you'll eventually appreciate too.

Perhaps Chloe goes back to Norway for a giant family reunion when she's seventeen. She meets cousins who look just like her and realizes that her white-blonde hair and pale brows and lashes connect her to those she loves.

Even if you *never* get that *aha* moment Chloe experiences, maybe you can get to the point where it doesn't possess you. You become neutral about it, and one day you wake up, live your life, and don't spend even one second of that beautiful brain power on it anymore.

It's possible! We promise!

QUIZ TIME

Which Comeback Style Is Most Like You?

We refuse to give any more quiz instructions.

1. "Is that your real hair?"

A. "It's really mine because I bought it."

B. "I don't want to talk about it."

C. "Is that a real question?"

D. "What an interesting question! I'd rather not talk about my hair with you, though."

E. "No. It's a wig. I have alopecia."

2. "You should get braces, bruh."

A. "Who needs perfect teeth when you've got this pitching arm, amirite?"

B. "Not everyone can afford braces."

C. "Did I ask?"

D. "It bothers me when you bring that up. Please don't say stuff about my teeth again."

E. "Eh. I'm cool with my teeth as they are."

3. "You really gonna eat that much for lunch?"

A. "Have you even had a nacho? Of course I am."

B. "I probably shouldn't, now that you mention it."

C. "And I'm gonna eat yours too."

D. "Everyone has a different appetite."

E. "I need the calories. I'm training for a weightlifting competition."

4. "Oh my God, bro is so short."

A. "Being average is over."

B. "I wish height was my only issue."

C. "And?"

D. "Talking about people's height as if it's something they can control is boring."

E. "He is, and he's the best forward varsity soccer's got."

5. "So where are you really from? Vermont, I know, but like before then?"

A. "Before when? Before I was born?"

B. "I dunno. I haven't done a genealogy thing."

C. "What a weird thing to ask."

D. "Not sure if you know this, but it's kinda rude to ask where someone is *really* from, because it implies I'm not as American as you or something."

E. "My parents were born in Vermont too. My grandma is Namibian, though, if that's what you're asking."

6. "Is it okay if I ask you how you ended up in a wheelchair? I remember you from kindergarten and you were walking!"

A. "I don't know, is it okay if I casually ask you about a very personal time in your life filled with trauma and heartache?"

B. "It's too much to talk about."

C. "Hey, I have an idea: No."

D. "It actually isn't okay. It's a story I only tell close friends because it's painful to talk about. Thanks for asking first, though."

E. "Yeah, it's fine. I was in a car accident. It sucked, but I'm good now."

7. "Isn't that a dude? Why's he in a dress?"

A. "Because obviously they've got style, darling."

B. "Don't stare. I don't want any attention on me."

C. "Why do you care? That's the question."

D. "Maybe it's time to broaden your perspective on gender."

E. "That's Alice, actually, and she likes dresses. Who cares?"

8. "Someone needs to tell Maddie to stop starving herself. She's like a hundred pounds."

A. "Someone needs to tell you to mind your own business. Let's make it me."

B. "Should we be worried about her?"

C. "Body shaming? Really? Grow up, Doug."

D. "Let's talk about self-love and acceptance instead."

E. "She's on cross country and in training for her first full triathlon too."

9. "He is honestly so ugly, though?"

A. "Huh. I was just gonna say the same thing about your mouth."

B. "Not as ugly as I am."

C. "All you do is yap, I swear."

D. "True beauty has nothing to do with a face, and he's a really great guy. Stop being mean around me."

E. "Guess that depends on who you ask."

10. "You look so good! I can tell you've lost weight!"

A. "Baby, I look good all the time, lost weight, gained weight, negative weight, exponential weight. Looking good is who I am."

B. "I never look good."

C. "Why are you obsessed with me?"

D. "Weight loss isn't a measure of looking good. Please don't compliment me on my body size."

E. "Thanks."

Answers

IF YOU CHOSE MOSTLY A'S, SARCASM IS YOUR RESPONSE TYPE. You're never one to let someone get to you. You just flip the whole conversation on them and leave them with a dusty taste in their mouth.

IF YOU CHOSE MOSTLY B'S, YOUR RESPONSES ARE A LITTLE BIT DISPIRITED. Maybe you tend to agree with the negative side of things, especially when it relates to yourself.

IF YOU CHOSE MOSTLY C'S, YOU TEND TO RESPOND FIERCELY. People being rude in front of you? Absolutely not. You tend to give it back and then some whenever someone comes at you with an intrusive comment or question.

IF YOU CHOSE MOSTLY D'S, YOU RESPOND WITH EMOTIONAL INTELLIGENCE. You're kind, constructive, draw boundaries, and tell people what you think in a positive way.

IF YOU CHOSE MOSTLY E'S, YOU TEND TO RESPOND HONESTLY. Not much bothers you, so when people make a rude comment or ask an intrusive question, you tend to answer anyway.

It's the Write Time

Time to spill! Pull up your Notes app on your phone or grab a journal and write what you want to say when someone makes an unwelcome comment about your body. Now write down an emotionally intelligent thing to say in the same circumstance. How could the effect of both messages be different?

"Wow, You've Lost Weight!" Discussion
QUESTIONS

1. How do you feel when people compliment your appearance? Does it impact the way you see yourself?

2. Pretend you're seventy-nine years old and have been sent back in time to talk to yourself today. What advice would you give your younger self about the way you look?

3. Come up with one thing to say after someone makes a comment about your body that doesn't sit right with you.

4. What part of yourself (inward or outward) are you really proud of?

5. Discuss a few different compliments you can give a woman that has nothing to do with how she looks. Now what about a man? Do the compliments change based on gender? Why or why not?

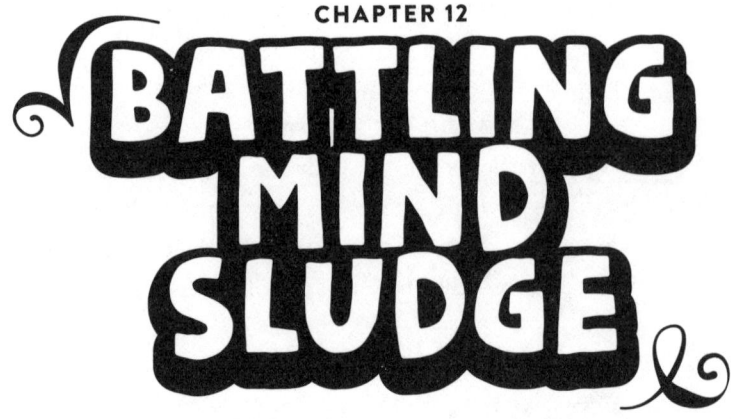

CHAPTER 12

BATTLING MIND SLUDGE

WE'RE SO MEAN TO OURSELVES SOMETIMES, AREN'T WE? OUR voices inside our heads can be worse than our worst critics on their worst days—and that's *bad*. Some of us call ourselves names we'd never use on anyone else. We might shame ourselves for normal human things or kick ourselves when we're down because we feel like we deserve it. Maybe we deny that we've ever done anything right in our whole lives, even when presented with bucketloads of evidence that we do, in fact, succeed occasionally.

If we could just chill with the self-loathing, that would be great, wouldn't it? But many of us don't. We get stuck mucking around in the sludge of our minds, up to our knees and sinking fast.

Those Sludgy Thoughts

Back when our ancestors were roaming the Earth, looking for raspberries to munch and creatures to hunt, we had a lot on our minds. Namely, staying alive.

That meant two things:

1. Remembering where we found the raspberries (a positive)

2. Watching out for Glerg and his willingness to bonk us on the heads with his club (a negative)

Which one was more important? Glerg, of course. The negative. Because if we forgot where we found the raspberries, eh. Oh well. There might be more on the other side of the hill. It wasn't an immediate life-or-death thing. But if we didn't watch out for Glerg, there goes our skull and whatever was in our pockets.

We remember the negative more than the positive because of our survival instincts, and young people remember more negative stuff than adults do. And yayyyyyyy, our brains can't tell the difference between major and minor negatives, so it shoves stuff like embarrassment and disappointment into the same pot as literal death. Your brain is trying to keep you alive when it says, "Hey, remember the time you were at bat and you struck out without even swinging? Cool. Replay that in your mind at midnight until you're twenty, because if you don't, Glerg's gonna get us."

Therefore, every negative thing becomes *VERY IMPORTANT* and *VERY MEMORABLE*—a sure sign that our brains are a real pain in the yee-haw.

No one wants to obsessively think about negative stuff daily, no matter what our brains are yapping at us to do. So, what do you do about it? Well, first, you identify the negative thought patterns. Then you remix.

ID the Sludge-Thought Patterns

Sludge thoughts, aka "negative thinking patterns," are ways we think about stuff that can convince us of things that aren't always true. Feast your eyes on this list to see if any of them sound familiar:

- **ALL-OR-NOTHING THINKING:** Everything is black or white. Good or bad. There's no gray or in between. You use words like *always, never, everyone, nothing, no one, all,* and so on.
  - *Everyone* has more friends than I do.
  - I'm *never* going to get better at this.
  - I'm just a *bad* test taker. That's how it is.
- **THE BINOCULAR TRICK:** You dial things way up or way down, making them more or less important than they actually are.
  - I can't believe I forgot my music. No one will ever let me live that down. (Dialing up anybody's care about your little mistake.)
  - He's just moody. He didn't *mean* to hit me that hard. (Dialing down the importance of a major red flag.)
  - They won't want to hang out with me, not after winning first place in state! (Dialing up someone else's accomplishments.)
- **DISQUALIFYING THE POSITIVE:** Good stuff doesn't count for some reason or another.
  - I only got on the team because my dad is friends with the coach.
  - She friended me on Insta, sure, but it was probably an accident.
  - I got an A on the test, but so did a lot of other people.

- **EMOTIONAL REASONING:** If you felt it, it must be true. Emotions = facts.
  - You're nervous on the first day of school and assume people are looking at you funny when they aren't.
  - You're feeling left out and assume the comments shared in your group chat are inside jokes when they're not.
  - You're feeling angry and falsely assume that someone cut the line to be an absolute toolbag, but they just didn't realize there was a line at all.
- **FORTUNE TELLING:** You assume stuff will turn out badly no matter what you do.
  - Why study? I'll fail anyway.
  - I mean, I'd ask her out, but she'll just say no.
  - There's no point in going. It'll be so boring.
- **MIND READING:** You assume you know what other people are thinking or feeling.
  - Welp, she didn't respond to my text, and that's because she hates me.
  - Love that he hasn't DMed me back. Must be talking about me with someone else.
  - Oh, her comment was super clear. She thinks I'm ugly.
- **NEGATIVE FILTER:** You obsessively think about one negative thing that happened, and it colors everything else around it (like a drop of ink in a glass of water).
  - Someone trolls one of your posts and it bothers you for months, to the point you don't even get on social media anymore.
  - A friend confesses that she doesn't like your boyfriend, and now you can't stop thinking about it every time you look at him.
  - Your cousin jokes about your new haircut and now you hate your hair.
- **PERSONALIZATION:** You blame yourself for things you have no control over.
  - Our team wouldn't have lost if I'd actually made my shots tonight.
  - My dad would stop acting that way if I were a better son.
  - My friend wouldn't have hurt themselves if I'd been a better listener.
- **SHOULDS:** You think about what you should or shouldn't do or be like, casting a lot of blame on yourself.
  - I shouldn't care about how many followers I have.
  - I shouldn't eat that.
  - I should have tried harder.

Recognize any of these? If so, great! You're on the right path. Identifying how we think can help us break these thought patterns. It can also help us understand when other people are saying things we don't need to believe.

From Tess to You

A negative thought pattern I've dealt with in the past
is Imposter Syndrome. That's when you feel like you don't
deserve what you have or don't deserve to be somewhere
you've literally been invited. I still have to work hard
to let go of that negativity. I have to tell myself all the time:
"Chill out. I was invited here. I belong!"

The Remix:
Let's Get Out of This Muck

We don't wanna stay here in sludge-thought land. Slimy things that leech onto your skin live here. If you need a few ways to pull your feet out of the muck, try these:

- **RECOGNIZE THAT THOUGHTS AREN'T FACTS.** Your brain isn't always spitting truths. It sounds odd to even think that, but our brains send untrue messages that mess us up all the time. We make assumptions, let our pasts color our viewpoint, and believe untruths others have told us.

- **EXAMINE THE EVIDENCE.** Try to back up your thoughts with facts. Will your dad stop acting mean if you clean your room? Or is it more likely that he'll do what he's always done regardless? Did she *say* she hates you and that's why she didn't respond to your text? Or are you just assuming things? What can you prove?

- **TOSS OUT EXTREME LANGUAGE.** Things are rarely *always* true, so get rid of words with a hard line like *never, always, everyone, can't,* and so on. *Everyone* isn't out having a good time while you're sitting at home. You're not a *bad* test taker. Maybe you haven't learned the skills for test taking, but giving yourself that name means you can't change, even though you can.

IT'S ALL IN YOUR MIND

Decide whether you're going to have a *growth mindset*, where you believe that your capabilities can be improved over time, or a *fixed mindset*, where you believe that you're as good as you can possibly get right now. Which one will lead you to greatness? Which one will give you more opportunities?

Let's try using a growth mindset to yank some of those thoughts out of the sludge. We'll remix them into something a little better for us.

THOUGHT PATTERN	SLUDGE THOUGHT	THE REMIX
All-or-Nothing Thinking	*Everyone* has more friends than I do.	I want to make more friends.
The Binocular Trick	He's just moody. He didn't *mean* to hit me that hard.	He's moody. He might not have meant to hit me as hard as he did, but hitting me is never okay, no matter what his intentions were.
Disqualifying the Positive	I got an A on the test, but so did a lot of other people.	I got an A on the test! I did great!
Emotional Reasoning	You're feeling left out and assume the comments shared in your group chat are insider jokes when they're not.	You feel left out but will assume the comments have nothing to do with you and instead will just invite a friend over to hang out.
Fortune Telling	I mean, I'd ask her out, but she'll just say no.	I'll ask her out and see what she thinks. She might say yes or she might say no, but I won't know for sure unless I ask.
Mind Reading	Oh, her comment was super clear. She thinks I'm ugly.	I could be reading it wrong. But even if she did mean it, it doesn't matter if she thinks I'm ugly. I like how I look.
Negative Filter	Someone trolls one of your posts and it bothers you for months, to the point you don't even get on social anymore.	You won't let someone else bother you. You'll block and move on.
Personalization	My friend wouldn't have hurt themself if I'd been a better listener.	I'm sad about what they did, but I'm not responsible for other people's actions.
Shoulds	I should have tried harder.	I want to try harder. I can't change the past, but next time, I'll give it my all.

Why Do I Freak Out?

Sometimes those negative thoughts turn into giant feelings and you find your-self freaking all the way out. You scream and slam your door. You tackle some kid you think has it coming. You cry hysterically. You think dark thoughts you'd never want to share with anyone. You feel hopeless, alone, isolated, out of control, and lost on a deep sea of churning waters.

Welcome to your brain, kids.

In the past, scientists called this wild reaction to stress *the amygdala hijack*, because they thought that a portion of your brain called the amygdala, or emotional center, would override your prefrontal cortex, the rational center, and make you fly off on some emotion.

Although that isn't 100 percent accurate (turns out the amygdala and pre-frontal cortex are homies), your emotions *can* make you do things that aren't so great.

Dr. Nika Douvikas, our pediatrician consultant, says that's partly because your frontal lobe (home of the prefrontal cortex) isn't fully developed as a teen, which is why rational thought sometimes gets punted off a bridge. But even for adults with fully formed brains, emotional intelligence can be really, really hard to come by.

That's why Dr. Douvikas says to practice these three steps when you're all worked up so you don't end up smashing your fist through a Taco Bell window when they get your order wrong.

Step 1: **LABEL YOUR EMOTION IN THE MOMENT.** When you're in the middle of *feelings* try to pinpoint a specific emotion. Sure, you're angry, but what if that big emotion is covering up disappointment, disgust, or jealousy? Or you're sad, but when you look deeper, you feel abandoned, lonely, or embarrassed? Now say it: "I feel disappointed." Not only will saying it help you process what you're feeling, it'll also help others understand you if you're brave enough to share.

Step 2: **PRACTICE MINDFULNESS.** It's okay to feel however you feel. Emotions aren't right or wrong; they just are. Accept them, and take some deep breaths, which can actually help you feel way less stressed, anxious, and depressed. Then take a second to be on your own so you can come back to yourself and figure out what to do next.

***Step 3*: REMIX SLUDGY THOUGHTS.** If you're stuck in one of those sludgy thought patterns, practice challenging what you think. Did you see the situation correctly? Have you misjudged anything? Made assumptions? Once you're calm, it's easier to judge things clearly, though very few people get this right all the time. Just saying.

STAYING IN THE GLOW

So how do you ward off some of those big, sweeping negative emotions to begin with? Dr. Patrice Berry, our psychologist consultant, says it can help if we train ourselves to focus on the *glimmers*—tiny moments that bring you that *ahhhhh* feeling of peace, happiness, or enjoyment.

We're not talking about an incredible vacation or your first kiss—those are big, fireworks things. We're talking about teensy flashes in your day that make you go, *Ah, that's nice*. Here are a few examples:

• The fresh, clean scent of a new bar of soap.

• The softness of your dog's fur.

• A parent lovingly ruffling your hair as they walk past you sprawled on the couch.

• Your favorite song popping up on your playlist.

• A friend complimenting your handwriting.

• Pulling a shirt out of the dryer and it's still warm when you put it on.

Dr. Berry says noticing those little things can help move the needle on your day. If your brain is swirling around something really bad, piling up all the glimmers can help push it out of the "everything is crap and I'm done" zone. It can even tip the entire scale back over to happy.

From Jess to You

Some of my glimmers just from today are giving my cat Smokey's nose a little boop, the soft lamps glowing in my apartment, and the scent of the new Unstoppables laundry beads when I did the laundry.

A Final Word on
Battling Mind Sludge

Your brain tries to keep you safe in the silliest way possible by making you focus on all the ways you've been hurt, but Dr. Berry says that while you can't avoid pain, you *can* avoid suffering. Suffering is what ya do with the pain you have. You can hold tight to the pain, keeping it clutched to your chest and never letting yourself heal. You can also hide from the pain by refusing to acknowledge it or distracting yourself away from it. But both of those methods make you suffer in the long run. Healing starts with understanding the mind sludge you carry, taking steps to change what you believe about yourself, and asking for help if you need it. Pain *does not have to break you.* There's a ton of support out there and likely a dozen people in your own life who would be delighted to help you if you asked.

Please see the Resources section of this book for places you can get help right this very second if you're more on the suffering side of things versus the "Oh hey, I have some pain" kind of things. We've got your back on this.

QUIZ TIME

What's Your Ideal Mental Health Day?

Last one! Have fun!

1. Pick a weekend activity:

A. Lying on the beach

B. Exploring a fair

C. Attending one of your games

D. Hosting a movie night with friends

E. Going to an auto care class

2. When you grow up, you could see yourself becoming a:

A. Park ranger

B. Graphic designer

C. Coach

D. Wedding planner

E. College professor

3. Your social feed is full of:

A. Travel vloggers

B. Sculptors

C. Viral dance trends

D. All your friends being goofy

E. Ads

4. Your personal pet peeve is:

A. People littering

B. AI art instead of human-made art

C. Having nothing to do all day

D. Being ghosted

E. Ignorance

5. Pick a song:

A. "Running Up That Hill" by Kate Bush

B. "Mirrorball" by Taylor Swift

C. "Hustlin'" by Rick Ross

D. "Friends" by BTS

E. "Even If It Breaks Your Heart" by the Eli Young Band

6. You wouldn't be caught dead:

A. Sewing a bumblebee on a sweatshirt

B. Playing beach volleyball with a group of sunbaked people in swimsuits

C. At a symphony, listening to a cello soloist

D. Without your phone

E. Slippin'

7. Pick a book based on the title:

A. *The Sun Is Also a Star* by Nicola Yoon

B. *Chloe and the Kaishao Boys* by Mae Coyiuto

C. *The Contender* by Robert Lipsyte

D. *Gravemaidens* by Kelly Coon

E. *The Edge of Anything* by Nora Shalaway Carpenter

8. Choose a color combo:

A. Forest green and coral

B. Royal blue and peach

C. Charcoal and sunshine yellow

D. Lavender and teal

E. Mustard and sage green

9. Which one lights up your life?

A. Fireflies

B. A desk lamp

C. Friday night lights

D. Warm sunshine

E. A spotlight

10. You're putting these on your feet:

A. Hiking boots

B. Clean socks

C. Running shoes

D. Whatever your bestie is wearing

E. Birks

Answers

IF YOU CHOSE MOSTLY A'S, SPEND SOME TIME OUTSIDE IN NATURE. Go for a hike in the woods or mountains. Host a picnic for your grandma on a blanket in the park. Fish in the neighborhood pond. Sled down a big snowy hill on winter break. Being outside can feel healing and revitalizing and give you a little bit of distraction from any stress too.

IF YOU CHOSE MOSTLY B'S, GET ARTSY. Grab your paint supplies and try a portrait. Sketch out a T-shirt design on your iPad or phone. Get a stitch kit and embroider the pocket of your jeans. Tie-dye a sweatshirt. Color. Sculpt a bottle out of clay. Make a necklace. Crochet a baby whale. You get the point. Artistry can take you away from negative thoughts for a while and let the creative side of your brain take over. Plus, making something can give you a feeling of accomplishment, which helps with confidence.

IF YOU CHOSE MOSTLY C'S, MOVE YOUR BODY. You're craving some endorphins, so go for a long walk in your neighborhood. Follow along to a dance, HIIT, yoga, bodyweight strength, Pilates, or Tabata class on YouTube. Ride a bike. Swim laps. Play a VR game that requires you to stand and swing. You'll feel invigorated, sweaty, and probably more than a little relaxed afterward.

IF CHOSE MOSTLY D'S, HANG OUT WITH YOUR FRIENDS. You need some together time, so have a few friends over and do makeovers, a game night, video games, or capture the flag. Volunteer together for a feel-good bonus. Go to an amusement park, bowling alley, the arcade, or the movies. Get ingredients and make your own pizzas or bake snickerdoodle cookies. Go watch one of your school teams compete. Real friends can give you a much-needed day off from stress and worrying. Laughing can also reset your mood.

IF YOU CHOSE MOSTLY E'S, LEARN A NEW SKILL. Challenge yourself to fix your own bike. Learn how to bake bread. Pick up the guitar your mom has in her room and teach yourself how to play a song. Find a poem and work out its meaning. Write your own. Download a language app and study Yoruba. Learning something new builds confidence and self-esteem, and you don't even have to be any good at it for it to work!

Draw It Out

Time to doodle! Get out some markers or crayons and a pencil. Get a sheet of paper and fold it in half.

On the top half, draw two characters, one that represents your inner critic and the other that represents the person who loves you the most—even if that's yourself. Color them with shades that show how each one makes you feel.

On the bottom half, write a conversation between the two of them, where the person who loves you most overcomes the inner critic.

On the back of the paper, draw your inner critic character getting smaller and smaller and smaller until they disappear into a tiny dot.

Battling Mind Sludge Discussion
QUESTIONS

1. Which negative thinking pattern has you in a chokehold? How can you weasel your way out of it?

2. How does the pressure of getting good grades or excelling in some activity like sports or clubs impact the way you talk to yourself?

3. Discuss the difficulties of balancing your own expectations with those of your parents or other interested adults. If you felt like you were in a really negative mental health space, which two adults could help you?

4. Name at least two glimmers you've experienced already today and why they give you a soft, fuzzy, "oooh, nice" feeling.

5. With social media an ever-present being in our lives, how can you maintain a sense of self-worth?

Conclusion Q&A

KELLY: Can you believe we're at the end? We did it! We put this whole book together.

TESS: No, I can't. It makes me want to throw up. I'm sad that we finished. Is that weird? I'll miss this.

KELLY: It's not weird. At all. I've gotten used to talking to you weekly. This has been a delight. A nice lil' glimmer in a day.

TESS: It really has.

KELLY: When I approached you about doing a book like this and we chatted about what it could be, I don't think I imagined all the stuff that we'd get into. Did you?

TESS: No. I wish I had this thing when I was younger. I learned so much through all the research!

KELLY: SAME.

TESS: And now we're done. Boo.

KELLY: Boooooo. But we can still end on a good note. Let me ask you a couple of the discussion questions from the book.

TESS: Let's do it.

KELLY: First one, and it might be my favorite. It's from the Find Your Fit chapter. If you could design a fashion line inspired by a book, movie, or TV show, what source would you use, and what would your clothes look like?

TESS: Oooh, okay. You're going to think this is so random—

KELLY: Let me hear it.

TESS: Haha, okay, but it's the *Magic School Bus* series and, specifically, Ms. Frizzle.

KELLY: HAHAHAHAHAHA—WHAT?

TESS: I told you, hahaha! But she's iconic! She's always been one of my favorites because she's always themed. If she's taking the kids to space, she's got planets on her dress. They're doing gardening? It's carrots or radishes or whatever. Ya girl *loves* a good theme, and so do I. Clothes should be fun and tell a story, and when I was younger I wasn't able to have very much fun with my clothes because I had a hard time finding stuff that fit me. So if I were designing a clothing line, it would be fun and bright and anyone could find clothes in their size.

KELLY: Okay, I *adore* that, actually.

TESS: Right?

KELLY: Yes. So, next question, from the Doing the Do chapter. What do you think people assume about you based on your hair?

TESS: Ummmm, that it looks good all the time? That I'm getting blow-outs 24-7?

KELLY: You're not?

TESS: Nope. I rarely style it straight. I wear my hair naturally curly 99 percent of the time. I'm in sweats and a T-shirt with a topknot on my head right this second.

KELLY: Same, though. Haha. Okay, next question from the Feed Me chapter: If you could only eat one cuisine from around the world for the next twenty years, which would you choose?

TESS: Oh, that's hard.

KELLY: The *most* difficult question of them all, actually.

TESS: Yeah. Well, if I had to choose, I'd say Italian, because there are so many options. You've got pasta. You've got salads. You've got cheese. You've got seafood. And it's all delicious.

KELLY: It is, isn't it? I went with Indian. I would eat chana masala every day. Or matar paneer.

TESS: Oh, I love Indian food too. Obviously, there's a bunch of different regions with their own flavors, but how are they all good?

KELLY: I know, they really are. And now I'm hungry. So let's move on to a question from the Bodies, Bodies, Bodies chapter so I can go have lunch. Haha! Which celebrity on social media has a positive influence on people's beliefs about themselves?

TESS: Easy. Dolly Parton. She always encourages people to be themselves and loves them exactly how they are. She's bursting with light.

KELLY: She really is. The vibes are vibing in the most beautiful way. And that's what true beauty is, don't you think?

TESS: Yeah. That's the inward beauty we've been talking about it. That kindness that shines out from someone who's just genuinely a good, kind soul.

KELLY: Which makes them beautiful on the outside too.

TESS: Exactly. A kind smile and sparkling eyes beats the hottest person on the planet.

KELLY: Truly. And having someone else label you as kind is the biggest honor. We talked about labels a little bit in the Call Me This, Not That chapter, mentioning that choosing labels for yourself should make you feel good. What are some of your positive ones?

TESS: I'd say empathetic, number one. If someone's going through it, I'm right there with them. Also nurturing. I'll mom everyone around me, no joke.

KELLY: Oh, absolutely same. If you're in my house, you're getting fed. Hugged. Sent home with a plate of food. Like everyone gets a big dose of momma Kell if they need it.

TESS: And I love that about you. I guess the last label I'd choose for myself would be funny?

KELLY: That's a yes. I don't know if I've laughed harder in my entire life than I have on the phone with you. We have *died* a thousand times.

TESS: We have. Hahahaha.

KELLY: And it isn't just me. People say that on social media to you too! You're caring, you're empathetic, you're funny as heck, which are all really nice. Are those the best comments you've gotten on social media? I mean people talk about your beauty all the time, but what's one of your favorite comments?

TESS: I got a good one recently when I was on a TikTok live. The commenter said that she's been following me since she was a teen and I've changed her life. I showed her it was okay to love herself exactly how she is.

KELLY: Oh woooooow.

TESS: I know. It was the highest honor. Somehow I've managed to positively influence her to love herself. What more could you ask for?

KELLY: Not much. That exact feeling is what we're trying to do with this book too. What's your ultimate hope for teens reading this?

TESS: I hope they treat themselves with the love they probably show others. That they understand that no matter what they're going through right now, it gets better. A lot of the crazy stuff during their teenage years is temporary or situational, and at the end of the day, they're in charge of their own destiny and happiness. What's yours?

KELLY: That's really good. I also hope that kids will love themselves from the inside out. That they'll know how much we care about them, and even if they don't feel good about who they are today, that can all change.

TESS: It can.

KELLY: Ready to say goodbye?

TESS: No?

KELLY: Haha.

TESS: If we have to.

KELLY: One last thing to say to the kiddos reading this?

TESS: You're amazing. All of you.

KELLY: You are.
YOU REALLY ARE.

All our love,

Kelly + Tess

Meet the Consultants

DR. PATRICE BERRY (she/her) is an experienced and compassionate licensed clinical psychologist in Virginia with over fifteen years of experience. Her private practice offers outpatient therapy for individuals, families, and children who have experienced trauma, adoption, depression, anxiety, and life stage issues. Dr. Berry is also a sought-after speaker, providing educational trainings on mental health awareness, integrating faith and mental health, and

the impact of racism on marginalized communities. She shares her expertise on social media platforms, including TikTok, YouTube, and Instagram (@DrPatriceBerry). Dr. Berry is also the author of *Turning Crisis into Clarity: How to Survive or Thrive in the Midst of Uncertainty*, which offers practical tips for managing life after adversity.

NIKA DOUVIKAS, MD (she/her), who often goes by Dr. Niky, is a board-certified pediatrician and loving mother of three young children. She completed her pediatric residency in 2019 and has dedicated the last several years to pediatric hospital medicine. Her journey in pediatric care extends beyond the hospital setting, as she works hand-in-hand with parents to navigate the intricacies of raising healthy and happy humans.

Dr. Niky has also embraced the digital realm, utilizing social media (@Niky.MamaMD) to extend her knowledge and experiences with millions of people. There, she provides education, support, and reassurance to a diverse following, including parents seeking guidance, teenagers navigating adolescence, and members of the LGBTQIA+ community, who deserve a safe space to be unapologetically themselves. Dr. Niky is not only a pediatrician but also a mentor, advocate, and ally to a large and continuously growing community.

Photo credit: Rachel Rubin

ANNA SWEENEY (she/her) is a chronically ill and disabled relational nutrition therapist and registered dietitian. She has dedicated her career to counseling, supervising, and consulting in the field of eating disorders. She is a certified eating disorder specialist and consultant as well as a certified intuitive eating counselor. Anna is the owner of a group nutrition therapy practice dedicated to anti-oppressive, fat-positive eating disorder care. Anna has spoken locally and nationally at numerous conferences and media outlets, is globally recognized as a resource in her field, and regularly communicates on social media as @dietitiananna.

TYM WALLACE (he/him) is a hairstylist who, in his fifteen years of experience, has worked with a plethora of top-tier celebrities such as Taraji P. Henson, Mary J. Blige, Serena Williams, Zendaya, Octavia Spencer, Yara Shahidi, Skai Jackson, Brandy Norwood, Gabrielle Union, Kelly Rowland, NeNe Leakes, Niecy Nash, Natasha Bedingfield, MJ Rodriguez, and Cardi B. These celebrities and more have been proud to have

Photo credit: James Anthony

their tresses "Tossed by Tym." After this Chicago native graduated from Dudley Beauty College, he made his mark in New York and Los Angeles, becoming a driving force in print, television, and film. Tym has worked with brands such as TPH by Taraji Henson, Carol's Daughter, Dove, Mielle Organics, and Tangle Teezer. His network credits include MTV, VH1, Bravo, BET, and WeTV, and his work has also been seen at Mercedes-Benz Fashion Week, Black Girls Rock, the BET Awards, *Project Runway*, and on countless magazine covers.

Tym has earned prestigious nominations for his exceptional work, most recently on *The Color Purple*, including the NAACP Image Award for Outstanding Hairstyling (Television or Film), Astra Award for Best Hair and Makeup, Critics Choice Award for Best Hair and Makeup, and Make-Up Artist & Hair Stylist Guild Award for Best Period Hair Styling and/or Character Hair Styling. With his gracious manner and breathtaking hairstyles, Tym pushes the boundaries of style and perfection.

Further Reading

Kelly's Self-Love Novel Recommendations

You're gonna love these! Each book ends with messages of hope and the main character's fierce determination to accept and finally love themself when they don't fit into society's expectations.

MIDDLE GRADE
(FOR AGES 8 TO 12 YEARS)

***ALL OF ME* BY CHRIS BARON:** Topics include body image, bullying, friendship, divorce, hiking, art, role-playing games, and preparing for a bar mitzvah.

***GARVEY'S CHOICE* BY NIKKI GRIMES:** Topics include body image, the pressure of sports, living up to parental expectations, bullying, athletic ability, astronomy, science fiction, reading, and school chorus.

***GENESIS BEGINS AGAIN* BY ALICIA D. WILLIAMS:** Topics include self-harm, parental substance abuse and gambling, colorism, verbal abuse, bullying, singing, talent shows, and friendship.

***GOOD ENOUGH* BY JEN PETRO-ROY:** Topics include eating disorders, mental health, therapy, hospitalization, body size, nutrition, drawing, running, friendship, and sisterhood.

***KARMA KHULLAR'S MUSTACHE* BY KRISTI WIENTGE:** Topics include body hair, interracial family dynamics, death of a grandparent, Sikhism, Christianity, and friendship.

***THE PRETTIEST* BY BRIGIT YOUNG:** Topics include body objectification, body image, popularity, beauty, bullying, girls banding together to fight social norms, inclusivity, and friendship.

SHORT BY HOLLY GOLDBERG SLOAN: Topics include height differences, dwarfism, death of a pet, friendship, art, finding role models, and self-discovery.

STARFISH BY LISA FIPPS: Topics include body image, shyness, parental bullying, classmate bullying, therapy, swimming, pet love, Christianity, and Judaism.

THE TRUTH AS TOLD BY MASON BUTTLE BY LESLIE CONNOR: Topics include literacy, body image, learning disabilities, synesthesia, excessive sweating, grief over the loss of a best friend, and classmate bullying.

TURNING POINT BY PAULA CHASE: Topics include body image, racial barriers, societal expectations, complex family dynamics, poverty, #MeToo movement, friendship, self-discovery, ballet, and Christianity.

YOUNG ADULT
(FOR AGES 12 AND OLDER)

DUMPLIN' BY JULIE MURPHY: Topics include body image, parental expectations, beauty pageants, bullying, friendship, romantic relationships, high school pressure, and small-town life.

FAT CHANCE, CHARLIE VEGA BY CRYSTAL MALDONADO: Topics include body image, parental pressure to lose weight, popularity, romantic relationships, jealousy, societal pressure, and first love.

FELIX EVER AFTER BY KACEN CALLENDAR: Topics include transgenderism, racism, art, college applications, social media bullying, catfishing, self-discovery, and romantic relationships.

FLYGIRL BY SHERRI L. SMITH: Topics include racism, World War II, women's equality, colorism, parental expectations, the military, ambition, and grit.

HALF LIFE BY LILLIAN CLARK: Topics include perfectionism, cloning, romantic relationships, first love, jealousy, divorce, redefining success, and societal expectations.

HERE THE WHOLE TIME BY VITOR MARTINS: Topics include body image, bullying, winter break, romantic relationships, introversion, friendship, and shyness.

HUNGRY GHOST BY VICTORIA YING: Topics include familial expectations, parental bullying, eating disorders, family tragedy, art, traveling to Paris, and the social media impact on mental health.

I'LL BE THE ONE BY LYLA LEE: Topics include saying no to societal norms, K-pop, singing, competitions, reality TV, media scrutiny, romantic relationships, body image, and self-discovery.

THE NEW DAVID ESPINOZA BY FRED ACEVES: Topics include body image, body-building, social media pressure, physical bullying, friendship, steroid usage, and obsession.

SCARS LIKE WINGS BY ERIN STEWART: Topics include scarring after a terrible fire, medical needs, disability, friendship, romantic relationships, beauty, and theater.

Resources

Immediate Help for Teens

- **988 SUICIDE & CRISIS HOTLINE** provides free and confidential emotional support to people in suicidal crisis or emotional distress 24 hours a day, 7 days a week, across the United States.
    - Chat: https://988lifeline.org
    - Call or text: 988
- **THE TREVOR PROJECT** provides free and confidential suicide prevention and crisis intervention support for LGBTQ young people 24 hours a day, 7 days a week, across the United States.
    - Chat: www.thetrevorproject.org
    - Call: 1-866-488-7386 or text: 678-678

Counseling

- **TEEN COUNSELING** provides online counseling for teens from ages thirteen to nineteen from licensed therapists in their state.
    - www.teencounseling.com
- **BETTER HELP** provides online counseling for teens and adults of any age from licensed therapists in their state.
    - www.betterhelp.com

Eating Disorders

- **PROJECT HEAL** provides life-saving support to people with eating disorders.
    - www.theprojectheal.org
- **NATIONAL ALLIANCE FOR EATING DISORDERS** provides life-saving support and a free hotline to people with eating disorders.
    - Call: 1-866-662-1235 9:00 a.m.–7:00 p.m. EST (Monday–Friday)
    - www.allianceforeatingdisorders.com

Food

- **NO KID HUNGRY** provides meals to kids around the United States 365 days a year.
    - www.nokidhungry.org/find-free-meals
    - Text Food to 304-304
- **FULL CART** provides food with dignity and discretion to families in need.
    - https://fullcart.org

Nutrition

- **EAT RIGHT BY THE ACADEMY OF NUTRITION AND DIETETICS** provides information about food, nutrition, and wellness for families.
    - www.eatright.org/for-teen
- **USDA MY PLATE** provides recipes, information, and interactive Alexa choices for teens about food and fitness.
    - www.myplate.gov/life-stages/teens

Social Media

- **HARVARD CENTER FOR DIGITAL THRIVING** provides resources for taking a balanced look at social media.
    - https://digitalthriving.gse.harvard.edu
- **AMERICAN PSYCHOLOGICAL ASSOCIATION** provides a health advisory for the use of social media in adolescence.
    - www.apa.org/topics/social-media-internet/
      health-advisory-adolescent-social-media-use

Research Notes

For a complete list of our sources, please scan the QR code or go to
www.hachettebookgroup.com/titles/tess-holliday
/take-up-space-yall/9780762489152/ to take a peek.

Acknowledgments

Tess's Acknowledgments

I'M GOING TO DO MY BEST TO NOT MAKE THIS A GIANT RUN-ON sentence or ramble too much, but there are so many people who made this book possible, and I gotta get them all! Like cute, lil', loving Pokémons! Haha!

First, I want to thank my amazing coauthor, Kelly, for making one of my wildest dreams a reality: creating this book for y'all. I truly manifested our meeting, and you captured my wacky thoughts and turned them into magical pages full of all the things I wish someone had told me when I was a young girl.

Thank you to my boys, Rylee and Bowie, for always being my biggest supporters. Rylee, you are brilliant beyond your years; Bowie, I can hardly wait for you to read this when you're older and finally give me credit for being the cool mom I am. Haha! You are both the best humans, and I'm honored to be y'all's mom.

Thank you to my team at Intention: Olivia, Erica, and Charlie. I love being part of such a magical group of folks who genuinely want to help me make the world a better place. Thank you for always believing in my big dreams!

Thank you to Jolene, my best friend and the reason I'm still able to pursue my dreams as a single mom. Thanks for being the big sister I always wanted and teaching me how to curl my hair, do proper skincare, and basically be an adult woman. And to our little/big sister Lizette, I hope wherever you are, heaven or a cool beach drinking out of a coconut, you know none of this would've been possible without you.

To Rainbow, my Cancer sister and birthday twin, you might be younger than I am, but you're exactly who I wanted to be when I grew up. Thank you for reminding me of why I was put on this planet.

To my partner, you know who you are—I always dreamed of someone covered in green flags who buys me gummy bears and appreciates and sees the person I truly am. You have helped heal the young girl in me that never felt lovable. You're my Kobe!

To the entire Running Press team, thank you for saying yes to our lil' book! To Julie Matysik, our editor, thank you for your guidance and patience. To all the hands behind the scenes—Frances Soo Ping Chow, Jess Riordan, Leah Gordon, Becca Matheson, Kara Thornton, Elizabeth Parks, Betsy Hulsebosch, Lindsay Ricketts, the Hachette Book Group Children's Sales team, and publisher Kristin Kiser—thank you for making this book into something I'm proud to show off.

To Dr. Patrice Berry, Dr. Nika Douvikas, Anna Sweeney, and Tym Wallace, I'm so glad y'all jumped on board with this. Trust and believe that Kelly and I would have *struggled* without your help!

Last but not least, thank you to my family and friends for loving me fiercely. My amazing moms, Beth and Lisa, who are truly my BFFs; my dad, Doug, the resident comedian; my little brothers (can you tell I'm the oldest?); Nadia, Junior, and Alya for showing up for me always; John for being the best dad to Rylee; Julianny for showing me the brightest parts of myself; Doreen for keeping the wonder and magic of my childhood dreams alive; JL for making me your muse a million years ago and changing my life; Farrah for making me a *Cosmo* girl and encouraging me to write more; and Debbie for helping future generations of young folks heal generational trauma and inspiring so much of this book. I love you all and am so proud to call you mine.

Finally, a HUGE thank you to my fans for hyping me and sticking by me no matter what. I wouldn't be where I am without you. And to any of you out there who never felt good enough or felt like you were "too much," thank you for still being here, because you belong.

Kelly's Acknowledgments

I WOULDN'T BE A VERY GOOD ACKNOWLEDGMENTS PAGE IF I didn't scream about getting to work with Tess Holliday on a book that makes me super proud. We did it, woman! Thank you for responding to my slightly unhinged DM on a random Wednesday evening and agreeing to work with me on this thing. You're a Pinterest board rockstar and a creative mastermind, and it's been my ultimate joy to do this with you.

Thank you to our editor, Julie Matysik, one of the best people I've met in publishing. You're so, so sweet and have made our writing shiny and bright. Thank you for lending us your incredible brain for this project. We stan your work (haha)!

Thank you to Kari Sutherland, my agent, who jumped into this project with me with the utter belief that Tess and I could do this, even when we doubted ourselves. You've championed me since 2017 and have been a dear friend I can count on for anything.

Thank you to the entire Running Press team who have put in long days and all their talent to turn this book into the beauty that it is. Thank you to VP and creative director Frances Soo Ping Chow for our drool-worthy cover and interior; to managing editor Jess Riordan and production editor Leah Gordon for your leadership; to the entire publicity and marketing team— Becca Matheson, Kara Thornton, Elizabeth Parks, and Betsy Hulsebosch—for running campaigns I could only dream about; to manufacturing coordinator Lindsay Ricketts for keeping the bus rolling on schedule; to publisher Kristin Kiser for your constant support (THANK YOU!!!!); and to the entire Hachette Book Group Children's Sales team for your superhuman efforts to get our books into readers' hands. I'm in awe of each one of you and am so grateful for your efforts.

Thank you to the experts who graciously offered us their time and talent. Dr. Patrice Berry, Dr. Nika Douvikas, Anna Sweeney, and Tym Wallace, this book would not have come to fruition without you. I hope you know how grateful we are!

Thank you, from the depths of my dark little heart, to my core team of fellow writers and critique partners who voted on subtitles and turns of phrase and made sure I didn't collapse into a ball of goo when things slid off the rails. That's you, Lillian Clark, Erin Hahn, Laura Taylor Namey, Dominique

Richardson, and Amy Christine Parker. A very special thanks also goes out to Sarah Glenn Marsh, Laura Sebastian, Shelby Mahurin, and Brigid Kemmerer for your kind texts and advice in the publishing world. To book influencer and bookseller Frank Chillura, you brighten my entire day and I'm honored to be your friend. Thanks for the TikToks that keep my mind *ahem* busy. ☺

Thank you to the booksellers, media specialists, and librarians who have supported me from day one, especially Kimberly DeFusco, Frank Chillura, Laura Taylor, Jennifer Dillon, Nicole Fincher, and Abby Cole. My job isn't possible without yours, and I appreciate all you do for authors.

Thank you to my fellow English teachers and friends—Calvin Dillon, Emily Kelley-Vona, and Eric Vona—for listening, giving advice, and lending me the best research books. You make me proud to have shared a profession with you!

Thank you to my family for your patience and sense of humor as I worked on this project. To my parents, Bill and Cindy Coon, your belief in me is why I'm able to create. To my sons, Brady, Kaden, and Brennan, I hope the messages in this book ring true, because for every hour my brain spent working on it, my heart was beating for you.

To my husband, Matt, I'll never be able to say thank you enough for the goddess-like way you treat me. I was lucky you kissed me that night on the beach.

And finally, to every reader out there (including my beautiful nieces, Natalie, Alyssa, Rhylin, and Skylar and my best friend Heather's daughter, Lily), I hope you realize just how spectacular you are right this very second. The world is better because you're in it.

About the Authors

Tess Holliday

AS ONE OF THE WORLD'S MOST FAMOUS PLUS-SIZE MODELS, Tess Holliday has been a pioneer in the body positivity movement. She broke boundaries with her *Cosmo UK* cover that went on to win cover of the year. She was named one of the most influential people by *Time* magazine and one of the top six plus-size models globally by *Vogue Italia*. Tess has graced many magazine covers, including *Nylon*, *People*, *Parents*, and *Self*.

Tess is the author of *The Not So Subtle Art of Being a Fat Girl*, an inclusivity consultant for global brands like H&M and Pinterest, and the founder of the viral #EffYourBeautyStandards movement, which encourages people to love themselves at every size. She was a keynote speaker at the inaugural World Eating Disorders Action Day at the United Nations and has been awarded the Global Changemaker Award by the National Alliance of Eating Disorders and the Inspire Award by Project Heal.

Tess's goal is to make sure there's a seat at the table for everyone and to give others the chance to make their dreams come true. She lives near LA with her sons and a couple of rowdy cats.

Photo credit: Bonnie Nichoalds

Kelly Coon

KELLY COON HAS MORE THAN TWENTY YEARS OF EXPERIENCE in writing, editing, and content development. She was the executive editor for Blue Ocean Brain and a high school English teacher, and she is a published fiction and nonfiction author. Her young adult fantasy novels, *Gravemaidens* and *Warmaidens*, were published by Penguin Random House in 2019 and 2020, and her two nonfiction test prep books, *ACT Strategy Smart* and *Ace the ACT*, were published in 2012 and 2017 by REA. Kelly has written and edited thousands of articles that have been published by Blue Ocean Brain, ThoughtCo, Scholastic, Microsoft, the *Washington Post*, and Scary Mommy, to name a few. In addition to her BA in creative writing and MA in English education, she's also earned a diversity, equity, and inclusion certification from Cornell University that guides all her content creation.

As someone who battled bulimia in college and watched her high school students in her classroom struggle to accept themselves, Kelly is passionate about promoting self-love. She lives near Tampa with her husband, three sons, and a feisty rescue dog named Roxy.

Photo credit: Erica Santo Photography